Creating

Brilliant Ideas

Alice Steinbart

Canadian Cataloguing in Publication Data

Steinbart, Alice
        Creating brilliant ideas

Includes bibliographical references and index.
ISBN 0-9685520-0-5

        1. Creative thinking.   2. Creative ability in business.
I. Title.

HD53.S74 1999   153.3'5   C99-900773-4

Published by Gildner-Reynolds,
        Winnipeg, Manitoba, Canada.

Cover photo by Faye McMaster, of McMaster Photographers, Winnipeg, Manitoba, Canada.

Acknowledgements

To Pat Nichol,

of Victoria, British Columbia, Canada.

Thank you Pat, for being my mentor.

To Mary and Bernie Lodge,

of Winnipeg, Manitoba, Canada.

Thank you for your comments and corrections.

To my cousin, Kurt Steinbart,

of New York City, United States.

Thank you Kurt, for your encouragement and
support.

To Gerri Thorsteinson,

of Winnipeg, Manitoba, Canada.

Thank you Gerri, for proof-reading.

Table of Contents

Chapter One

Introduction

Pick a word and write the first word you think of, then your next thought, and the next:

finger nail → nail clippers → cutting → cutting the grass → smell of freshly cut grass → smell of roses → summer is coming → warm sun → relaxing in the sun.

Everyone will come up with a different set of associations and with an ending something other than relaxing in the sun. If I change one of the associations, the smell of roses → romantic interlude, I am now off in a new direction, with another ending.

Introduction

Our society sees creativity as happenstance, a bolt from the blue. We see it as the province of artists, scientists, and geniuses, for the Shakespeares, Mozarts, and Einsteins. "I'm not creative," we say. These beliefs are wrong and I will prove it. This book sets out 24 specific tools which are catalysts. They will get your thinking going in a different direction, to create brilliant, new, valuable ideas.

Ouch.

This was not the first time Sir Isaac Newton saw an apple fall. But this time, something was going through his mind that connected with seeing the apple fall. Something that sent his thinking off in a new direction, which eventually lead to him formulating the law of gravity.

Where do ideas come from? How can you create new ideas at will? Ideas come from the associations you have, from the connections you make. If you want a new idea, get a new association. Associations come from other associations and from the stimuli you receive and from the associations you make to those stimuli. One association leads to another. Change the association and you will get a new thought, a different idea. Try it. Pick a word. Write down the first word you associate with it, then the next, and the next, until you have a dozen. That last word will be something so different from the first, you will wonder what possible connection could there be. But the sequence is there, one from another. And someone else, starting with the same word will have completely different associations. They will come up with a completely different idea. An example is shown on the opposite page. The first concept is finger nail and the end result is relaxing in the sun. How in the world are those two connected? But the connection is there, from one idea to another.   This is how ideas are created, from the stimuli we receive and the associations we make.   Change the association and you will end up with a new idea. One thought will lead to another.   You think of this which reminds you of something else which leads to yet another association. When you start, you have no idea where you will end up. Use the tools in this book to start a new association, to get a new idea.

What do you think of the idea of everything being possible for you? All the abundance of the world available to you. Of being brilliant, capable, overflowing with ideas. Creating ideas gives you this potential.

History is the story of our rise from ignorance, squalor, an animal-like existence, to whatever we choose to make our lives. From no awareness we could control anything, to understanding we control the most important parts of our lives. We came from there to here by creating ideas. This is a "how-to" book. How to create brilliant new ideas, at will. For creativity is not luck or happenstance. It's a learnable/teachable skill. Creating ideas has given us everything we have, from our clothes, food, houses, to our beliefs about ourselves and our world. Someone thought up how to do it or how to view it. Someone created each idea which resulted in what now surrounds you. The alphabet that gives you the words for this book. The paper on which the words are written. The distribution system which got this book into your hands. The money to buy this book. Jobs to earn your money. Your community, your country where you live and work. Everything started with an idea. You can now create new ideas, using the tools in this book, to move ahead in your business or career, increase your competence, make you more money, propel you beyond your blocks.

What is Creativity?

Creativity is thinking something
you have never thought before,
even if someone else has.

It does not have to be original.
Only original for you.

It does not mean
you have to come up with an idea,
no one has ever thought of before.
Only that you never thought of it before.

It does not have to be new in all respects.

An improvement to an existing idea

is creative.

Using an existing product

in a new way

is creative.

Everyone is creative. Yes, you too. If you have ever used a paper clip for something other than clipping papers, you have been creative. This is improvisation and you do it a lot more than you think.

When we think of creativity our first image is the artist, the musician, the inventor. This is only a part of creativity. There

When you use a paper clip
for something
except clipping papers,
you are creative.

are many types of creativity.   There is the

improviser. The latch comes off the door. I can screw it back in but the hole is too big. I don't have wood-filler. I could stuff something else in the hole in the meantime to give a foundation for the latch screw to grip onto. I could move the latch, higher up or lower down. If I do not use the latch, how else can I keep the door shut? And the ideas, the possibilities keep coming, one after another. One seems to lead to another.

Apollo 13 is a story of improvisation. An oxygen tank exploded, destroying part of the spaceship. The three astronauts shut down the command module and moved into the lunar landing craft. But the carbon dioxide filters in the lunar module could handle only two people for two days and not three people for four. Carbon dioxide approached lethal levels. They needed to use the filters from the command module, but they were square and the slots in the lunar craft were round. It was a classic case of fitting a square peg in a round hole, with only the material on board. They improvised a filter from amongst other things a plastic bag, duct tape, and the cover from the flight plan. It worked.

You have the same ordinary tools available to you, and you use them, to be innovative. You do not need to be a scientist or an artist. You are creative in your own way. Even those whom we recognize as original, Shakespeare, Mozart, Einstein, were creative in their field. Shakespeare could not have composed music like Mozart. Mozart was no Einstein. Einstein could not write Shakespeare. So there is no point in comparing yourself to a well-known creative, and say "I am not like that". You have your own creativity and you are as different from Einstein as Einstein was from Shakespeare.

Creativity exists, not just in the scientific or artistic, but in every field, every activity. There is practical creativity, such as a person coming up with a new recipe. "Hmmm, I wonder what this would taste like if I tried cloves instead of cinnamon." Or a new lay-out for storing things. Would it be more efficient if I put this here instead of here? Or a new design for clothes. What if I cut the pattern this way instead of this way? Would it be easier to sew or more comfortable to wear? After all, at one time our clothes consisted of wrap-arounds. Cloaks and togas were wrapped around. Foot coverings were wrapped around the feet and tied. Who thought of cutting two legs for trousers and stitching the seems together. Definitely easier to wear. The first person who tried putting wooden boards on their feet to ski over the snow, was a practical creative.

There is concept creativity, such as Gandhi with civil disobedience and Martin Luther King, Jr. with civil rights. It's the Women's Movement. Or those who turned us into a non-smokers society.

If you look around, everything you see and everything you know about, was created by someone. Who thought of the wrist-watch to replace the pocket watch? And who thought of putting rollers on chairs so we could move around easier? Who thought of selling by catalogue? Who thought of shopping centers, franchises, and supermarkets? Who thought of cheques? And then

Don't let
baldness
go to
your
head.

Creativity is common.

credit cards? And debit cards? Who came up

with the idea of aluminum baseball bats? Who first designed T-shirts. Then who thought of putting funny remarks on T-shirts? And who thinks of those sayings?

These creations are not Nobel prize winners. I do not need to be a scientist, engineer, inventor, researcher, or have gone to university to come up with ideas like these. They are simple, yet smart. Simple enough that even I could have thought of them. Ideas that make money and make life better. Ideas like the ones you are going to create.

Everyone is creative. Including you.

How To Be Creative

Almost everyone who writes about creativity, writes as if it is some mysterious ingenuity that comes to us from time to time and to some more often than others. Even those few who feel creativity can be turned on treat it as "getting into the mood" or "getting into the flow", by doing strange things like standing on your head or putting on a puppet show, or colouring. And while this is similar to one of the tools in this book (The Silly Tool), it is only one tool.

This book sets out 24 specific tools that will jar your thinking into a different direction, so that you will come up with new ideas. The tools fall into eight categories:

The Preparation Tools
The Start-up Tools
The Organizational Tool
The Right Brain Tools
The Left Brain Logical Tools
The Left Brain Lateral Tools
The Borrowing Tools
The Improvement Tools

If we try to come up with answers to our problems without using the tools in this book, we usually re-hash the same old tired ideas we have tried or heard of before. Creating new ideas gets us beyond these blocks, into that dazzling world of WOWS. The tools in this book make that possible, even simple.

Each tool is designed to propel your mind in a new direction. Use a tool and you will get a series of answers. Use another tool on the same question or problem and you will get different answers. Go back to that tool at another time and you will get still more new answers. Ideas are endless. One leads to another. The tools in this book get you started and give you direction. So that creating valuable ideas is no longer happenstance or luck.

Why Creativity?

"I don't need creative ideas," growled the C.E.O. "What I need is more time and money."

All of us need something and everything starts off as an idea. Ideas can create more money, more time, better relations. But some ideas are tired, worn-out, ineffective. Too often people see a problem and come up with the same old solutions. Creativity produces that magical answer that is just right for you. Taking you to the next level instead of re-hashing the standard ideas. You need money. You have probably heard all the traditional ideas on how to get more. What are the new ideas that work better? You need more time. You have taken the time-management courses. Are there new ideas, better ones that answer your problem?

Creativity is valuable. Ideas are powerful. Everything you think, want, see, do, or have, started with an idea that had to be created. All your ideas, your concepts, from democracy, to civil rights, to tolerance, all were thought of, created by someone, passed down to you and accepted or changed by you. Everything you have, all the physical comforts, the consumer goods, all started as an idea that someone created, someone thought up, from the job you have, to what that job entails, to the value you put on it, to the way you view yourself, your self-esteem, to what you want or expect from your family, what love is, and isn't, how you expect others to behave towards you. Creativity is the starting point for everything. Creativity is powerful, basic, and important.

Creativity is the cutting edge of the future. Do you want to keep up? Then you need to learn how to be creative, at will. If you want something better, you will have to know or do something differently. You need to be creative.

Creativity will make you more competent, more capable. You will get ideas that make your life easier and better.   Whatever blocks or obstacles stand in your way, you can create ideas to move beyond them. You will find answers and solutions to your problems.

Your creativity is your natural ability. You already have it.   You may simply have not recognized it or used it. Since it is already there, it's easy to access through the tools in this book. With creativity, you can take charge of your life. You are able to produce idea after idea.   Some ideas will work, be good, and some will not. The ideas that work will make your life better. They will be valuable. A problem comes up. You look at the tools you have. You pick one and use it to solve your problem.

Creativity is a life skill. A life skill is any ability which makes my life easier or better. From minor enhancements to major ones.   Being optimistic or positive is a life skill. Being able to balance my cheque book is a life skill. Using my anger effectively to get what I want instead of being out-of-control is a life skill.

Creativity for the joy of it. Who knows where my ideas will go. What I will end up with. What ideas will come tumbling out. All types, silly, useful, far-fetched, and the breath-taking. The kind that make you stop, almost in awe. Often astonishingly simple. Where you say, "Why didn't I think of that before?" The kinds of ideas, where in the back of your mind, you are impressed by yourself for thinking of that. There is a pleasure, an excitement, a sense of fun and challenge to being creative. So why creativity? For the joy of it.

The Emerald Rule of Creativity

There is a solution to everything, usually several solutions.

This is the Emerald Rule of Creativity. Emerald being green and green being one of the colours associated with creativity.

There are two parts to this rule:

1. There is a solution to everything. When you believe everything is possible, you will be more open to new ideas and less likely to give up. You think "even if I don't know the answer, it does not mean there is no solution. It simply means I don't know the solution. Yet". We are in the Information Age. It's been estimated our

knowledge is doubling every seven years; maybe even faster in some areas. So someone may have the solution and I do not even know about it. Or they may have the information, the idea, the trigger which will lead me to find the solution. Or maybe the technology needs to catch up; we need to make advances in some other area before we can solve the problem here. There is always a solution to everything.

2. There are many solutions. Being copiously creative is an important part of being successfully creative. The more ideas you create, the more likely one of them will be a powerfully good idea. You only stop looking if you have decided to spend a specified amount of time creating. You never stop because you have run out of ideas or you cannot think of anything more. When you get to that place, use the tools in this book. Go back to the tool box and pick another tool, including perhaps The Incubation Tool. At the very least, you can improve the ideas you have created.

In addition to many ideas, look for diversity. If I hand you a sheet of paper and ask you for a dozen uses, you can tell me I can write a letter on it, use it to take notes, to photocopy, make a sign, draw a picture, make a Valentine's card, and so on. But there is no variety in these ideas as they all use the paper for writing. But if you said I could use it to wrap something up, then this is a different category. Or if I wad it up and use it to practice basket-ball, this is a different category again. There is richness in your ideas.

We have all heard examples of "it can't be done thinking". We laugh at some of the things that have been said:

"Everything that can be invented has been invented" Charles Duell, U.S. commissioner of patents, 1899

"[Television] won't be able to hold onto any market it captures after the first six months. People will soon get tired of staring at a plywood box every night." Darryl Zanuck, head of 20th Century-Fox, 1946.

"Nobody now fears that a Japanese fleet could deal an unexpected blow on our Pacific possessions...Radio makes surprise impossible". Joseph Daniels, former U.S. Secretary of the Navy, 1922.

"What use could this company make of an electrical toy?" Western Union's President William Orton, rejecting Alexander Graham Bell's offer to sell his telephone to Western Union.

"Radio has no future." Lord Kelvin, mathematician, physicist, and former president of the Royal Society, 1897.

Characteristics of a Creative

Some characteristics enhance your creativity. You can cultivate these traits. You can still be creative without them, but you will be more creative with them.

When Benjamin Franklin sent up his kite in an electrical storm, with a key tied to the string, he did it because he was curious. Curiosity is a characteristic of a creative.

So is being flexible, open-minded, willing to try new things. The book-store owner who first put a coffee-shop in her book-store, was willing to experiment.

We think people resist change. In fact, people are much more open and flexible now than in past centuries. Look at all the changes in the last 100 years. We have accepted cars, airplanes, telephones, computers, credit cards, radio, television, and the list goes on. If people resisted them, these innovations would not have happened. We would not have bought them or used them. What we think is resistance to change may be uncertainty or hesitation, even nervousness, because of a learner's awkwardness.

Sometimes ignorance is an attribute of creativity. Experts are more likely to say, "that won't work", and are less likely to experiment. Assumptions and rules are like boundaries you have to jump. They are limitations, restrictions, which hold you back. So do not be deterred by lack of knowledge. It may be your cutting edge.

Attitude is key to creativity. Creative people believe they are creative. When I see myself as unable, I become unable. Negative thinking like "I've never been any good at that" or "I'm not creative", blocks creativity. Thinking "I wonder what would happen if...", and "I could try that", promotes creativity. You develop this belief by admitting you are innovative and by noticing when you are. Be a believer, believing you are capable of creativity, and you will become more so.

Leonardo da Vinci was a Renaissance Man, of vast knowledge and many interests. He filled notebook after notebook with creative ideas. Having varied interests or experiences will enhance your creativity. One creativity tool is to borrow something from one field and apply it to another. If you have an interest in music, you will think in terms of synthesis, sound, and rhythm. If you are a salesperson, you will think in terms of marketing, benefits, features, and financing. If you are an athlete, you will think in terms of strength, endurance, movement, breath control, exercising, and food intake. If you combine these interests, you will come up with something new.

Pre-school children are creative. They make up stories, have vivid imaginations, draw in wild colours, try things out. They do not know something is not suppose to work, so they do it. Children love laughing and playing. Laughter leads to creativity. If you can be child-like, playful, or funny, then you will be more creative.

Interest, enthusiasm, motivation nourish creativity. You love the challenge, the excitement of the new, the discovery. So cultivate your interests. Find what stimulates you. You will become more creative.

Persistence is a necessary characteristic if you use The Stubborn Tool, and also when it comes time to getting your creative idea accepted.

Tools

The tools in this book are catalysts or triggers to get your mind thinking new ideas. Without tools, we would live like animals. How could you cook without an oven, or pot, or fire-pit? How could you write without a pen, or printer, or all the tools needed to make paper? Where would you live without the tools used to build your house? Just as we need tools to live our lives as we do, we need tools to create ideas. All our predecessors who created all that we have, used the tools in this book to do so. Without calling them tools. This book is the "aha", the click. So we now see what was there all along, but we did not know. Where we used to think creativity was happenstance or luck or a gift to the brilliant, we now know that it is controllable. You can be creative, at will. You, whenever you want, can create ideas, workable ideas, useable ideas, brilliant ideas. This book shows you how.

There are 24 tools and you can use one or several to get your creativity flowing. You may start with one or more of The Preparation Tools and then move onto one of the other tools, and finally end up using one of The Improvement Tools. The more tools you have, that you know how to use, and are willing to use, the better you will do and the easier your job will be. The "Creating Ideas" tools can be compared to using gardening tools. If you want to garden and your only tool is a shovel, you are going to find it difficult to rake. Some tools, like a seeder, are specialized, and can be used only for one chore. Other tools can be used for more than one job. Like a hose, which you can use to water, fertilize, or clean something.

And so it is with the "Creating Ideas" tools. Some tools are specialized and meant only for certain types of problems. Other tools are general. Some tools are similar to others. Just as a shovel and garden fork are similar as they are both meant for digging. Some tools work best when used in combination with others; like a hose and a nozzle. Some tools, like a riding mower, require more skill, and you need practice or experience to use them. If you decide you do not like a tool, such as a hoe, as hoeing is such back-breaking work, and you decide not to use it, then your garden will show it. If you decide you do not like some of the "Creating Ideas" tools, that you are a left-brain person, and you do not like the right-brain tools, you will be less creative.

The tools are there to help you. Your garden and your creativity will flourish when you use them all, properly.

Nothing Comes from Nothing

Everything is connected. No idea is ever entirely new. It always builds on something, or puts two or more existing things together, or uses existing ideas in a new way. Nothing comes out of a vacuum.

Let's try proving this wrong. What are some new inventions? The airplane. The Wright brothers did not invent the gas engine, but they used it on their plane. They did not invent the wheel, nor the propeller for the Kittyhawk, but they put all the components together in the right way to make the airplane.

Einstein's theory of relativity definitely was a new idea. But he (and we) had to understand a number of concepts, ideas, before he could come up with his theory. We had to have the concept of mass and energy. There was a time in human history when people never thought about mass or its attributes. They thought in terms of the four basic elements—fire, water, earth, and air.   If scientific theory was still at that stage, Einstein's work would have been quite different.

To discover America, Columbus had to have a sailing ship capable of crossing the

Atlantic. If navigation was still at the canoe, row-boat, or raft stage, then Columbus could not have done it. By Columbus' time, ships were bigger, faster, and more efficient. Sailors were going on longer and longer voyages. They ventured out into the Atlantic, out of sight of land, to the Canary Islands, eighty miles offshore, the Madeira Islands, 390 miles out, and the Azores, 800 miles from Europe. The Portuguese had sailed all the way down the African coast and around the Cape of Good Hope. Columbus needed to know the Orient was there. He needed to know what Marco Polo and other traders knew.

So whatever new discoveries or theories we come up with, they are always built on what we already know or have. Everything is connected. There are no orphans. We either take existing ideas or things and expand them. Aluminum foil is an example of this. Aluminum was first mass manufactured in the 1920's. We saw aluminum pots and pans, boats, and siding. Reynolds Metals was looking for a better foil than the tin sheeting available. What else could be thin and pliable for wrapping? Could aluminum be stretched thin enough? They experimented, made changes, and finally came up with aluminum foil in 1947.

Or we take existing ideas or things and modify them. Elevators came from hoists. People have been using hoists for centuries to lift loads to heights. But no one thought to modify hoists to lift people to higher floors until Elisha Otis in the 1800's. Once the elevator was invented, sky-scrappers became possible. Before that the tallest residential and office buildings were no more than five stories, as people did not want to walk up more stairs than that.

Or we take existing ideas or things and put them together with other ideas or things. A modern example is combining the television with the computer.

Or we take existing ideas or things and use them differently. The microwave oven came from the microwave used for radar developed in the Second World War.

Or we take existing ideas or things and make some changes to them. Potato chips came from French fries. One customer complained the fries were too thick. The chef cut them thinner. Still the customer complained. The chef, in irritation, cut them paper thin. The guest loved them and so we have potato chips.

Everything is built on something else.

Chapter Two

Creativity
Right and Left

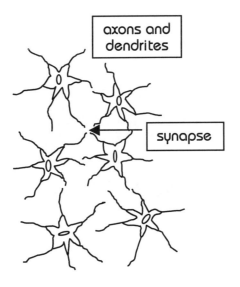

axons and
dendrites

synapse

Brain cells showing
the axons and dendrites
with the synapses between.

Electrical Impulses

Where do ideas come from? All our ideas, our thoughts, are electrical impulses coursing through our brains. They follow paths, from cell to cell, along tentacle-like dendrites and axons, jumping the gaps between, called synapses. The impulses travel out from the dendrites, across the synapses to the axons. Each electrical impulse leaves its mark, like a set of footprints in the snow. So the next electrical impulse is more

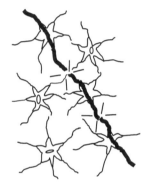

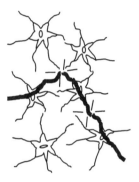

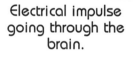

Electrical impulse going through the brain.

Electrical impulse taking a new path.

likely to follow that channel just as the next person is likely to use the path that is already trodden. The more ideas, stimuli, experiences you have, the longer the dendrites and axons extend, linking to new brain cells. The more your thoughts travel the same track, the longer and thicker those dendrites and axons grow. The more you use your brain, the smaller the gaps between the brain cells become, and the stronger the channels are imprinted.   It becomes self-reinforcing. How do we get out of this rut?

All creativity comes from triggers. Something has to trigger us. Something has to send that electrical impulse coursing through our brain down a different path. Every trigger comes either from a stimulus or an association. Stimuli come from what you are seeing, hearing, touching, smelling, or tasting. Stimuli lead to associations, which lead to other associations. Thoughts, ideas always come from associations.

There are always electrical impulses going through your brain.   Only when you are brain dead do they stop. Even while you sleep, you are receiving stimuli. There are sounds in the night; you feel the bed against your skin. All these become electrical impulses traveling through your brain. Each stimuli leads to an association which leads to another association.   You never know where you will end up from one association to another.

I'm driving to work.   I see a sign announcing an event.   I remember going to the event last year with my cousin. I have not talked to him for a while and I wonder how he is doing. I should call. Or I am driving to work. I see the same sign. I do not remember that sign being there yesterday. I wonder when they put it up? I think my memory is going. Or I see the same sign. Is it August already? I am not ready for school starting. I have to.... So one trigger, the sign, can lead to many associations. Associations can go in different directions. When you change directions, you will have a new thought.

One stimulus can trigger any of a number of associations. I can choose which association I am going to make, or I can just let it happen. Most of us, most of the time, just let it happen.

But with the tools in this book, we can direct our thoughts.

"Creating Ideas" tools will spark your mind into a new direction. Make you think of new ideas. Tools which will get your mind to jump the boundaries you have imposed, to leap a different synapse. And who knows where it will go. What is down that path? And what divergences in the road your thoughts will come across. What ideas will you create?

So let us begin our quest into creativity.

Flow

Flow is change, eventually. Even the

Flow
Passion or Interest
Concentration or Focus

Everything changes, things we think are permanent. Mountains are worn down into hills. Rocks become sand. The sun will eventually burn out. Stars and galaxies, explode or implode. Everything changes. And what is change but flow?

Change or flow cannot be stopped. You are always in flow, as is everything else. But flow can be blocked or diverted. A river of water can be dammed. But the dam will not stop the flow. Some water will spill over the top. The rest will be diverted outwards, to form a lake, or back to elongate the lake. The direction of the flow is blocked, but the flow, change itself, is never stopped. It can only be slowed down or diverted into a different direction.   Nothing can stop change. That's good news for creativity.

Flow is also a state or feeling. It can be compared to water flowing.   It's fluid. It's like floating.   Flow occurs when ideas come easily, effortlessly, when everything clicks.   When you become so engrossed in what you are doing, you lose track of time, of what is going on around you. You have a feeling of energy, that everything is working. It happens when you forget the end result, and there is only the here and now. When you get caught up in the present moment. Where what you are doing or thinking becomes all-absorbing. When it becomes fun, a challenge. When you give up the demands, worries, gottas, and have-tos, and forget the obsessiveness, the anxieties, the problems. When you get out of the adrenaline-driven behaviour, where you deal with life by pushing, trying to do too many things in too little time. As when you get off work at five and have to be home by six, ready to eat. But you have four chores to do on your way home. You have to get some groceries, pick up the dry-cleaning, go to the hardware store, get some gas.   You cannot possibly do it all in an hour, along with your travel time, but you have to, "you gotta". You're pumped up. You're really moving. You're driving like a maniac, weaving from lane to lane, running the lights. This is adrenaline behaviour.   In its positive form, it leads to highs, being energized, getting things done.   In its negative form, it is stressful and leads to frustration, irritability, and anger. It is not flow.

There are two requirements to get into flow:

1. Focus or concentration. There must be no distractions. When you are passionate about something, and your attention is concentrated on it, you are in flow. Take the focus away and you have lost flow. Will-power will not get you into

flow. Will-power, discipline is a distraction. You will get focus either by dealing with the distraction, or by substitution, where the new interest becomes so compelling that it overrides the distraction, so that you are now focussed on the new interest.

2. Interest or passion. If you are concentrating on something, but it has no interest for you, you are not in flow. You are merely intent. Take away passion and you have lost flow. Passion can sometimes be enough to get you past the distractions. But if the distractions are too strong, passion alone will not do it.

Distractions include worry, disorganization, aches and pains, confusion, low self-esteem, anything that takes your mind away from your focus. So when you want to get into flow, find your passion, eliminate whatever might distract you. The flow will come. And doesn't it feel good?

Right-brain and Left-brain Creativity

Those few who have dared to fathom where creativity forms, either perceived it as a right-brain phenomenon or a left-brain genius. The reality is we use both our right and left brains to be creative.

Right brain thinking unfolds in pictures, images, and feelings. It is nonverbal and wholistic. We get the complete idea. It does not come in parts or stages or step-by-step. It's just suddenly there and we do not know how we did it, or where it came from. It's like a flash of insight, the "aha", the eureka. It seems to be uncontrollable. Either you have it or you do not. It comes when you are sleeping, dreaming, day-dreaming, meditating, while in a relaxed state, or in an altered state, such as driving on automatic pilot, or while listening to music.

Left-brain creativity is verbal, sequential, and rational. Something you can understand, figure out. Once you have found your answer, you can turn around and see where you came from and explain how you did it. It is not a sudden flash of insight, but is describable.

Everyone has preferences. If you think of yourself as logical, you might see right-brain thinking as "airy-fairy", "new agey", mushy. If you are inclined to be a right-brain type, then a left-brain style does not interest you. But there are advantages to moving beyond your preferences. You may be surprised by your ability to think on the other side of your brain. A person who is open and flexible will be more creative. We think of scientists as objective, rational, logical left-brain creatures. Yet they use right-brain tools.

Thomas Edison reported that he would take frequent naps and keep a pen and paper by his bed, so he could record ideas that came to him as he dozed off to sleep or as he was waking up. He was using the right-brain Relaxing Tool.

August Kekule, who discovered the structure of the benzene molecule, said the answer came to him as he was falling asleep by the fire. He saw snakes dancing in his imagination, forming a circle and eating their tails. From that he realized the structure of the molecule had to be closed and circular. Like Edison, he used the right-brain Relaxing Tool.

Einstein tells of being bored and watching the clock, daydreaming, imagining travelling on a beam of light to the clock and then past it. Does time slow down? It started him thinking about the speed of light and time, which eventually led to his theory of relativity.

Both right and left brain creativity work, for all of us, whatever our preferences may be. Right-brain creativity is controllable. There are right-brain tools you can use that will spark ideas for you. You will be a more effective creator if you are willing to use all of the tools. Test yourself. Test your openness, your willingness to be flexible. Try the right-brain tools if you are left-brain oriented and the left-brain tools if you are right-brain. Do it several times. Push past your biases and the unfamiliar. Then see if you like it. The more tools you have and use, the more brilliant you will be.

How to Use the Tools

Everyone who created an idea, got to their creativity by using one of the tools in this book. They probably did not recognize they were doing so.

The person who came up with the idea of dinner theater may have used The Booty Tool, putting together the ideas of restaurant and live theater. Or maybe they used The Detective Tool and asked "How else can I attract more people to my restaurant?", or maybe they used The Check-up Tool and asked, "What would make my restaurant better?".

Perhaps The Change Tool gave rise to the debit or cash card, by changing one characteristic of the credit card.

Did Charles Darwin use the what if... question of The Explorer Tool to formulate his Origin of the Species theory?

When Ignaz Semmelweis discovered that doctors could prevent childbed fever by washing their hands between patients, he used The Hawk-eyes Tool of paying attention

So how do you use the tools?

1. Suspend your judgement. Every idea is acceptable and must not be judged at this stage.

2. Prepare the question, using The Detective Tool and The Flip Tool.

3. Then pick another tool and use it to produce as many ideas as you wish.

4. If you are stuck, use The Silly Tool, or The Humour Tool, or go back to The Detective Tool and The Flip Tool, or pick another tool and use it.

5. Once you have your ideas, go to The Improvement Tools, pick one and see how you can make your idea stronger.

6. Now decide if your ideas are workable or unworkable.

Chapter Three

The
Preparation
Tools

What are your mind traps?

The Preparation Tools

Creativity starts with preparation. How you word your question or perceive your problem will lock you into a box just as surely as if you stepped into a trap.   The answer you get always depends on the question you ask. If the question is "how do I increase sales by 10% in 90 days", the answer is not going to be "drinking and driving don't mix". Unbreakable glass proves it. The President of Corning, while visiting the research and development lab, complained "Glass breaks. Why don't you do something about that?" The lab took this to mean find unbreakable glass.   If the President had asked "why can't you make unbreakable glass", the researchers might have spent three months on a report explaining the properties of glass and why it breaks. But he did not ask "why can't". He asked, in effect, how do you make unbreakable glass.   The researchers looked for a different answer and eventually developed Corelle ware.

So creativity starts with preparation. What question am I going to ask? How am I going to word it?   How else can I word it?   What assumptions am I making?   How are my assumptions limiting my creativity? The question points towards the answer.

We start with The Preparation Tools, move onto another tool or tools, and end up with The Improvement Tools. There are three Preparation Tools:

1. The Detective Tool
2. The Flip Tool
3. The Rebel Tool

Ask Questions.

Who?   What?

When?   Where?

Why?   How?

Is this the right question?

The Detective Tool

Questions are good triggers. Triggers jolt your thoughts into new directions. They get those electrical impulses coursing through your brain to jump to a new channel, to come up with different ideas. This tool gets you to ask questions you may not normally ask. It prompts you to ask the basic questions who, what, when, where, why, and how. Each question is just a short-hand, representing a whole series of questions. The "what" question can represent engagement ("What am I going to do about it") to disengagement ("What would happen if I do nothing"). Some examples of different questions are:

Who:
> Who needs this?
> Who else can use it?
> Who has the information to help me?

What:
> What is the problem?
> What needs to be done?
> What else can be done?
> What am I trying to do?
> What do I need to know?
> What do I want to end up with?
> What other ways can I do this?
> What are the alternatives?
> What do I want to avoid?
> What are the requirements?

Why:
> Why is this a problem?
> Why now?
> Why am I working on it (as opposed to someone else)?
> Why do it this way?

Why fix it (change it)?
Be careful of "why" questions, as they lead to "because", meaning "you can't", which gets you stuck. This is most obvious in "why can't I...?" questions.

<u>Where:</u>
Where is this a problem?
Where is this going to be used?
Is there anywhere else it can be used?

<u>When:</u>
When is this a problem?
When do we need it by?
When is it going to be used?
When else could it be used?

<u>How:</u>
How else can I use this?
How does this work?
How else could it work?
How else can I do it?

<u>How Many:</u>
How many people want/need it?
How many times do they need it?
How many do I need?
How many times does it work?

<u>How Much:</u>
How much will it cost?
How much will it be used? (How can I increase the use?)
How much is it needed? (How can I increase the need?)

<u>How To:</u>
> How do I use it?
> How do I explain it?
> How do I sell it?
> How do I find it?
> How do I fix it?
> How do I store it?
> How do I take it apart?

To construct the question and ask it in the right way, you need to summarize all the information you have. For example, my washer and dryer manufacturing business has remained static for the last three quarters—from January to September. During the same period the economy has grown by 1% and no new technology has come onto the market. There are no new competitors and none have left. Both the wholesale and retail prices have remained constant and the cost of manufacture has increased .5%. I want to increase my profits.

My list of questions could include:

Who uses my washers and dryers?

Who else could use them?

What is the most profitable part of my business?

What more can I do to make it more profitable?

What do users want from my machines?

What could I do to my machines to motivate non-users to buy them?

What can I tell non-users to convince them to buy my machines?

What makes my machines less desirable?

Where else can the washer and dryer be located? (They are usually in the basement or utility room which involves a lot of walking. Change that.)

Why do non-users not have a washer and dryer? (This can include money, space, time, need, access to vendor, repair shop, delivery, power, or water).

How else can the machines be used? (Snuggling into warm sheets or wrapping a dryer-hot blanket around yourself could be another way to market dryers. Could we have smaller dryers for this purpose in the master bathroom? Would fluffing in addition to warming be an attractive option? Could dust-removal for allergy sufferers be a marketing tool?)

How can I wash and dry fabrics which are not now washable or dryable?

How else can I sell it (apart from department stores, furniture stores, and appliance stores)?

How else can I explain it, fix it, store it, take it apart? How can it be folded up to take less room? (Since the bulk of the size is the drum which is empty when not in use.)

Now I have my rough draft of questions. I can pick several, or I can follow a theme, or I can pick one question. Then I proceed to The Flip Tool to check if my question is correctly worded. From there I pick another tool to jar my mind into a different direction, to create new ideas. I take these new ideas and use The Improvement Tools to make the solutions even better. The Detective Tool has started me on my way.

All creativity comes from getting your mind out of its pattern of thinking.

Change the Question
to the Opposite.

Make It:

Positive   Negative

Neutral

Specific   General

The Flip Tool

How you ask your question will lock you into a certain direction. It will pre-determine your answer.

If I ask the question--
What makes the dog bark?
        I will get theoretical answers.
The dog is upset, scared, reacting to being
        tied up.
The dog is undisciplined.
The dog needs a dog psychiatrist.

If I change the question to—
Why can't I get the dog to stop barking?
        I will get "it can't be done" answers.
I can't get the dog to stop barking because
        the neighbours are too stupid,
        the city does not care,
        that's the way dogs are.

If I ask instead—
How do I get the dog to stop barking?
        I will get "can-do" answers:
I can talk to the neighbours.
I can report the dog to the city.
I can get information from a dog trainer,
        which may give me more answers.

The purpose of The Flip Tool is to twig your mind into other possibilities of phrasing the question, so your thinking will go in a new direction. You can make the question positive:

How do you get the traffic to flow better?

Negative:
>
> Why is the traffic not flowing?

Neutral:
>
> What ideas can you come up with on traffic flow?

You can change the question to the opposite.
>
> How do you stop the traffic flow?

You can make the question general.
>
> What makes traffic flow?

Or specific.
>
> How does the use of stop signs compared to traffic lights affect the flow of traffic?

You can use different verbs, different words.
>
> What makes traffic speed?
> What makes buses prompt?
> What makes trucks accelerate?

You can break the question into steps or stages.
>
> Traffic starts.
> Traffic stops.
> Traffic slows down.
> Traffic speeds up.
> Traffic gets heavy.
> Traffic is light.

This may change your focus from movement to rhythm.

With some questions, you can look from the inside out.
>
> When you are in the middle of traffic, what does it look like? Is it different from looking from the outside in?

Or you can look from the top down.
> If you took an aerial view of the traffic flow, what would you see?

Or you can look from the bottom up.
> From the point of view of the road, what does the traffic flow feel like? How heavy are the vehicles? How much resistance or friction from each? How long are they? How much room between vehicles, both the sequential and the parallel distances?

Or you can start with the end result and work backwards.
> The destination of this vehicle is point B. What are the ways it can get there? In addition to different routes, there may be different methods, from being flown there, to bulk transportation. If we have ferries transporting cars and their occupants across water, what about a land equivalent (land ferries), loading cars in bulk to a common destination, from which they fan out. If traffic is a problem in Los Angles, what about the possibility of a shuttle train, taking cars and occupants back and forth from one part of the region (San Bernardino) to another (Santa Monica). Similar to a subway for vehicles. Is this an alternative to building more freeways or more lanes on a freeway?

So this tool has jarred your thinking into new ideas. You are asking questions you would not have thought of without it. If you use The Improvement Tools, you may find some of your ideas could be workable.

Write out your assumptions.

One is wrong.

Make a wrong one.

What are the rules?

Break one.

The Rebel Tool

The purpose of The Rebel Tool is to get you to open your eyes to what you take for granted. It gets you to rebel against your assumptions and rules.

"If you always think
what you have always thought,
you will always get
what you have always got."
Unknown.

Most of the thoughts and ideas you have today are similar to the thoughts and ideas you had yesterday. How do you get different thoughts? The Rebel Tool is your catalyst. There are three ways to do it:

1. list all your assumptions, your beliefs, your expectations of what will happen, or what needs to be done, or how it has to be done. Then pick one. Make that assumption, belief, or expectation wrong. It cannot be done that way. What are you going to do now?

2. instead of listing your assumptions, deliberately make a new and wrong one. How does that affect how you view your problem? Where does this new concept send your ideas?

3. instead of listing your assumptions, list all the rules. Now break one.

This is going to force you into thinking in a new way. It shatters your routine mind-set and thrusts you into fresh ideas.

This is the tool to help experts climb out of the box that their expertise imposes on them. Experts know what is acceptable and what will bring them ridicule or diminish their standing in their colleagues' eyes. They know what works and are not prone to experimenting or challenging the norm. This tool forces them to do that.

Let's see how this works:

You are a banker and you are wondering what creative ideas you could come up with to improve banks. What assumptions do you make?

Assumptions:

Banks lend money.

People use banks as a safe place to keep their money.

Banks issue and cash cheques.

Banks are regulated.

Banks charge interest on loans.

Banks impose service charges.

Banks pay interest on savings.

Banks make their profit on the difference between the interest they pay on savings and what they charge on loans.

Now pick an assumption—banks charge interest on loans. What if it was illegal to charge interest on loans? So how can the bank make money? What about a percentage of the profits derived from the loan, or if the loan does not produce profits, then a percentage of any profit produced by the business. The greater the risk, the greater the percentage. Or the greater the amount loaned, the greater the percentage. Or the longer the time loaned the greater the percentage. The idea of profits sparks the idea of taking shares in the company instead of profits, or maybe taking a combination of both.

There are some attractions to the profit-based loan, just as there are some drawbacks. It may be useful for some types of loans, but not others. Profit-based loans can pay more than interest-based loans. But if there is a default, will the bank lose more on a profit-based default than on an interest-based one? The mortgaged property will cover defaults for either type of loan. But with an interest based loan, the bank will probably receive at least some interest payments before default. But would there be enough time for a bank to receive some profit payments before default?

In any event, you now have new ideas. You can use The Improvement Tools and work through the drawbacks in these ideas and see if they can be made workable. The Rebel Tool has done its job of jarring your thinking in a different direction.

The alternative to listing your assumptions and picking one to question, is to make a wrong assumption. Either way, you will be forcing your mind in a different direction. Different directions produce new ideas, different results. You will come up with creative ideas. From there you go to The Improvement Tools to see how you can make the ideas better.

"If you have a penny and I have a penny and we exchange pennies, you still have one cent and I still have one cent. But if you have an idea and I have an idea and we exchange ideas, you now have two ideas and I now have two ideas."

Unknown.

Chapter Four

The
Start-up
Tools

The Start-up Tools

Getting going. Sometimes the ideas just flow. But when they do not, The Start-up Tools will get you moving.

The Start-up Tools are used both at the beginning and anywhere along the way. At the beginning, they close down the critic, quiet any anxiety ("Can I do this? I'm not creative."), and stop the distractions ("I've got to solve this."). Now you are able to give free reign to your thinking.

Along the way, if you ever get stuck, go back to The Start-up Tools. They start you free associating, clearing out the blocks, so you move from one idea to another easily.

There are two Start-up Tools:
1. The Humour Tool
2. The Silly Tool

Laugh at your
favourite comedian.

The Humour Tool

The Humour Tool gets you into a creative state of mind. All ideas, thoughts come either from stimuli (seeing, hearing, feeling) or from associations. One association leads to another. New associations lead to new ideas. Humour is based on association/disassociation. The joke starts off in one direction. The punch line suddenly disassociates from that idea and pulls you over to something completely different.

"Have you been moved to a branch office?"
"No, it's not really a branch. It's more like a twig."

The first line brings up a picture of a large company with several offices. The second line disassociates to a tree.

"Keep your nose to the grindstone and your feet on the ground... and you'll not only wear off your nose, but you'll have a heck of a time getting your pants off."

The association starts seriously with the well-known cliche to work hard and disassociates to how silly the metaphor is.

If you listen to humour for a time, you will, by osmosis, get into an associative/disassociative mind-set. You will be moving quickly and easily from one association to another. One study on humour and creativity was based on one group of participants watching a half hour comedy show. Immediately following the show, they came up with more ideas in the same time period than the second group which did not have any humour warm-up. Humour gets you into the mind-set you need for creativity. It lightens up your inner critic, allowing ideas to flow. Humour will start you off in the beginning and will get you going again, if you ever become stuck in the middle of the session.

Be Bizarre.

The Silly Tool

The purpose of this tool is to:

1. Get you started, both at the beginning of the creativity session and when you get stuck. It brings an association, a silly one, that will lead to another association, which may not be as silly, which leads to another one, which may work.

2. Silence the critic, the judge, we have in our heads, telling us the idea is stupid, or will not work. We already know it will not work; it's silly. It's meant to be silly.

3. Put you at ease. Silliness is associated with having fun. It's o.k. to say whatever you want. You are allowed to be silly.

4. Open your mind and make you flexible. If you think or say this silly thing, then anything is possible or permitted.

What is the stupidest, most far-out, dumbest, craziest, weirdest, nuttiest idea you can think of? Of course it will not work. It's not meant to. It's meant to get you started. Because one association leads to another, which leads to another. Eventually it may lead to a workable idea.

This tool is the most potent method of jarring your mind out of that complacent rut it's in, of getting you out of that ordinary, common-place, regular, repetitive thinking. You must deliberately think of crazy ideas. Now you are someplace else. Where is it going to take you? From a stupid idea, which brings to mind another idea, which may not be so crazy, which leads to yet another idea, which may be not too bad, which sparks another idea, which may turn out to be useful. The Silly Tool definitely forces your thinking in a new direction, which leads to new ideas, creative ideas.

There are two related techniques to The Silly Tool. The first is exaggeration—I am going to build the most efficient distribution system of retail goods in the world. You can order anything you want, from appliances to clothing, and get it the next day, customized to your specifications. Once I have made this decision, now I must figure out how to do it.   The exaggeration has got me thinking along a different line.

The second related technique is wishful thinking. I wish I had a billion dollars. I wish I could flap my arms and fly. I wish I could be relaxing on a warm sandy beach right now. Again, once I say it, my mind could leap to how to do it. It takes me in a different direction, from which new ideas arise.

Let's try an example using The Silly Tool. I start with the question,

How can I improve public parking?

Now what are some of the crazy ideas I think of:

No parking is allowed anywhere.

Parking is allowed everywhere all the time.

Parking costs $1,000.00 per minute.

Cars are designed to explode if they stop longer than 5 minutes.

You will lose ownership of your car if you leave it unattended.

All buildings are razed and everything is paved into a parking lot.

Parking spaces are assigned by lottery.

You are assigned a parking space at birth and it never changes.

Now I pick one—parking spaces are assigned by lottery---and list all the thoughts, ideas, and associations as they tumble out.

I can sell it, transfer it, trade it, or rent it out. Even non-car owners get a space. Businesses might want to rent or buy spaces near them.

Space owners might consider time-sharing. Maybe parking should be based on need. What if it is based on a combination of need and time-sharing? What if you are not assigned spots, but streets or general areas?

What if parking was more regulated for the purpose of organization and planning? What if you had travelling parking spaces, like the truck that loads up seven cars for transportation to car dealers, or like the trailers we have for temporary accommodation or office spaces. How tightly packed or arranged could this temporary parking be? Like being on a shelf with a crane to bring the cars in and out.

This would be useful for shopping centers for Christmas shopping or special events parking. If in three parking spaces you parked one temporary parking trailer, which could shelf six cars, then you are getting three more spaces, or double what you had. Here I draw a diagram to get a mental image of how it could work.

PARKING TRAILERS

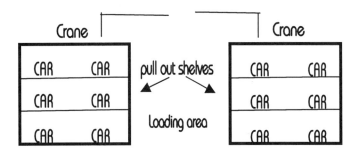

This leads to the idea of changing parking lots so there are no aisles. You drive into the small loading area. A crane lifts your car to a vacant space, and when you want to leave, it picks up your car and brings it to the loading area. I draw another diagram to get a picture of how it might work.

PARKING LOT

car				car	
		car		loading	
car				area-- crane	
	car				car

entrance

Now pocket size parking lots can hold maybe double the cars as there is no space lost for driveways. (About three weeks after I wrote this, I noticed that someone else not only came up with a similar idea, but actually built a parking garage. It's not unusual for people to come up with the same or similar ideas independently of each other.)

Then an idea occurs that with the use of the crane, we could park cars on the flat rooftops of commercial buildings. In particular this may work for buildings 1-3 stories high. A car drives into the loading area; the crane on the roof picks it up and deposits it onto the roof. When the driver returns, the crane takes the car off the roof and deposits it in the loading area. The owner drives off. This could give parking spaces to businesses that may now have little or none.

In any event, you now have come up with several possible workable ideas. You can continue on as one association leads to another, so there are still more ideas to be gleaned from this line of thinking. You may end up going off in a totally different direction, having nothing to do with stacking trailers or cranes. Or you can take the ideas you have now and use The Improvement Tools to see if you can make them workable. So The Silly Tool has done its job of jarring your mind out of its rut and into a new direction.

The person
who has the most
solutions
is the person
who will have
the most successes.

Chapter Five

The
Organizational
Tool

The Cranial Nerves

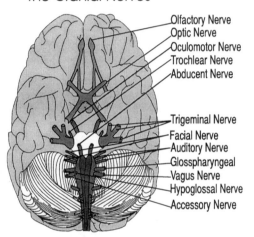

Olfactory Nerve
Optic Nerve
Oculomotor Nerve
Trochlear Nerve
Abducent Nerve

Trigeminal Nerve
Facial Nerve
Auditory Nerve
Glosspharyngeal
Vagus Nerve
Hypoglossal Nerve
Accessory Nerve

Mind Map

The Organizer Tool

This tool forces you to organize your thoughts, write them down, one after another. One thought leads to another, which may lead to a new idea. You may have heard of this tool under the name of clustering or mind-mapping. It works because one thought will lead to another. The disadvantage is there is no built-in assurance that the ideas that are sparked are new rather then a listing of old ideas. As a result, this tool is not as powerful as other tools.

How do you do it? Write the question or problem or key word or phrase in the middle of a blank page. Then around this write down all the thoughts, ideas, and associations you have to it. Circle these ideas and connect them to the main word with a squiggly line and each sub-topic to the idea before. When you have a new association start with a new circle, connected to the central idea. Since creativity comes from triggers, from associations, what you are doing is writing down all your associations to that idea. It's the association which sparks another association that generates the creative ideas. Ideas come tumbling out and suddenly I am someplace else. I have made a connection I never expected when I started.

Colours, drawing pictures or symbols, ($, ☺ , ♡) all spark different associations, getting your mind, your thinking going in new directions. These aids keep the flow going.

I decide to draw a mind map on how to encourage kids to stay in school, and I get the following ideas:

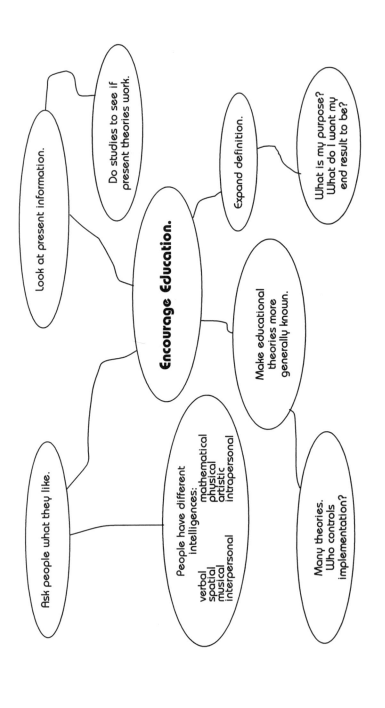

Chapter Six

The
Right-Brain
Tools

Every problem
is an opportunity
to be creative.

The Right-Brain Tools

Of all the types of creativity, right brain is surrounded by the most myths. Some people think creativity only comes from the right brain. In fact there is both right-brain and left-brain creativity.

Some people think you have to be artistic to be creative. However, artistic creativity is only one type of creativity.

Some people think right-brain creativity is silly, mystic, "airy-fairy". But right-brain creativity is real, verifiable, and occurs in all of us, we just do not notice it. Machines can trace those electrical impulses running through your brain, whether it is on the right or left side, whether you are being creative using right-brain or left-brain tools.

Some people think you access right-brain creativity by drawing with your opposite hand, or dancing, or dressing up in unique clothes. That may work, but you do not need to use these methods.

Some people feel right-brain creativity is not controllable, it just happens. But right-brain creativity occurs when we take specific actions. There are tools which will get you into right-brain creativity. We control our thinking. We just do not know it.

There are two Right-brain Tools:
1. The Relaxing Tool
2. The Incubation Tool

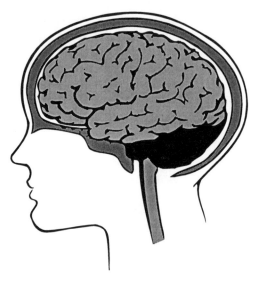

Slow down your

brain waves by

sleeping/taking naps

meditating

relaxing

The Relaxing Tool

Right-brain creativity is the stuff of dreams, of a quieter consciousness. Those electrical impulses criss-crossing your brain have a rhythm and frequency which we have labeled brainwaves. Researchers have found there are different tempos

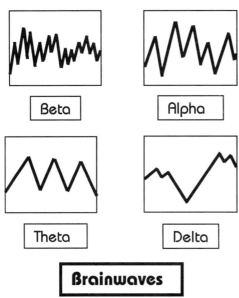

Beta

Alpha

Theta

Delta

Brainwaves

to these waves. Beta is the awake, active stage. The state you are hopefully in now. Left brain creativity is at this level. As your brain waves slow down, before going to sleep, or just on waking up, or when you are deeply relaxed, meditating, listening to lulling music, you are in the alpha state. Theta waves are even slower, as in dream sleep. Right-brain creativity occurs at the alpha and theta levels. Non-dream sleep, the slowest of the brain waves, is delta.

We all go through each of these levels everyday. As our brain waves slow down, our electrical impulses are open to a new direction, travelling through different brain cells, jumping across different synapses, making different connections and associations, to create new thoughts and ideas. But most of us never notice this. We are in too big a hurry to get going, to wake up, to get to work. If we stopped at this state and sat quietly, we would get ideas, creative ideas.

Screeeeech.   "Another red light". I think, "That newspaper article is right. All the lights are out of sequence." As I look down the street, I see alternate red-green lights.   "This is stupid," I decide.   "Why don't they synchronize these lights? Computers are capable of doing that."   My mind leaps to that customer yesterday who thought I was capable of tracking her order.   "And she's right," I reason, "we can program the computer to do that."   So here I am, daydreaming at a red light, and my thoughts have gone from red light annoyance to work solutions.   Now there's a creative connection.

Our associations, our thoughts, string together like miniature lights on a Christmas tree, one leading to the next.   As my eyes follow the lights up the tree, why do they move to the blue light instead of to that yellow one? I could trace a pattern in any direction, just as my thoughts flit from this brain cell to that. They could as easily cross over to a different brain cell, forming a new idea. If I pay attention when my mind has slowed down, I will capture these new thoughts.

This tool can be used when you have some free time: you are stuck in traffic, travelling on a plane or train, waiting in the doctor's office. Take some deep breaths and let your mind drift. Daydream. See what comes. The Relaxing Tool lets your mind drift like a boat on the river. Drifting boats end up at different land falls from steered boats.   The Relaxing Tool allows your mind to go in a different direction, to come up with new ideas.

When we sleep, we dream, whether we remember our dreams or not. If we are willing to take the time, we can learn to recall these dreams and the ideas they trigger.   Dreams are often strange, disjointed. They give us associations and connections that we never make in our waking moments. Connections we can use to create new ideas. But you have to capture them as soon as you wake, before getting up or thinking other thoughts. Get them down on the paper you can keep by your bedside.

You access your right-brain creativity everyday. So if you want something new, different, creative, if you want to get out of your left-brain rut, pay attention to what's going on in your head, when your mind is at your lower brain wave frequencies.

Incubation.

Work on an idea.

Then leave it.

Listen for an answer.

The Incubation Tool

Sleep on it. Isn't it odd how this works? Yet we have all had that experience. You have a problem. You work on it and get nowhere. So you put it to the back of your mind and move onto other things. But that idea is still there, in the back of your mind, incubating. And then suddenly the answer comes to you.

There are many electrical impulses or thoughts coursing through your brain at any given moment. So when you put an idea into incubation, your brain is still making connections, associations, there in the background, without your conscious awareness. Just as your brain is aware of what's going on right now in your left foot, processing the touch sensations it is feeling or the co-ordination of walking, all without your being consciously aware of it, so too your brain is processing this idea you are incubating at the back of your mind. Your mind is always working, clicking along, checking with this, cross-referencing with that, until you make a connection, that electrical impulse which travels along a new path, to come up with an idea that pops into the front of your mind. We have all used The Incubation Tool.

The process of incubation is spend time thinking about your problem, so that it becomes fixed in your brain. (The more often an idea is thought, the thicker and longer the dendrites and axons of the brain cells in that thought pattern grow, and the more deeply ingrained the channels for the electrical impulses become. A more deeply imprinted idea in incubation will be worked on more often.) Then leave it to incubate. Periodically check in to see if there is an answer. Checking in is simply paying attention to your thoughts. Not trying to create any solutions, but rather noticing what is there, below the surface in your subconscious. It may take time, but if you listen, it should come. You know from experience that it works.

Chapter Seven

The Left-Brain Logical Tools

It is important
to make the distinction
between
what cannot be done
and
what has not been done.

The Left-Brain Logical Tools

Left-brain tools fall into two categories: logical and lateral. The logical process is step-by-step, one idea leads to another, in an orderly sequence, until you figure out a solution. You ask questions, observe, experiment. You try this. It does not work. You try something else. No, not that either. O.K., how about this?

A pictorial drawing of logical thinking.

We are taught to be logical and it is highly respected. Science and technology rely heavily on left-brain logical thinking. Technological and scientific discoveries often come in two parts. One part is the hard slogging of proving, observing, testing, refining, manufacturing, getting out the bugs, which may be interspersed with the need to create new ideas on "what do I try now?" and the other part is the dramatic finding. Penicillin is an example. The first part of the discovery was a serendipity accident. Alexander Fleming was growing staphylococcus bacteria in petri dishes. One culture got contaminated by a rare type of penicillin mold. It killed the bacteria. Fleming was trying to grow the staph, not kill it, so he could have thrown that culture out as a failure. Instead he paid attention, got curious, and started observing. This was the exciting discovery. But the second part of actually identifying the mold, isolating it, growing enough of it, purifying it, testing it, took years of work. It took The Stubborn Tool of keeping at it, trying this, then this, then something else. That is why Fleming shared his 1945 Nobel Prize in medicine with

Ernst Chain and Howard Florey. Fleming found the mold, but Chain and Florey found how to purify it into a drug. Fleming used The Hawk-eyes Tool of paying attention; Chain and Florey used The Stubborn Tool of persisting.

Western society relies heavily on this creativity. There are three tools that stimulate left-brain logic:

1. The Stubborn Tool
2. The Explorer Tool
3. The Break Apart Tool

Ideas are endless.

Persist.

If it does not work,
try something else.

The Stubborn Tool

This tool encourages you to keep on. We have learned many new things by trial and error. This tool is the most familiar to our rational, empirical Western thinking. We use logic to deduce the theory, then test it with experiments or observations, to see if what we have developed works. If it does not, then we make changes, try something else and test it again. We do this all the time. You have to get financing for your project. Financing is never a simple matter of you ask and you get. Instead you get creative. What would it take to convince the financiers to lend you money? You calculate the amount you need, the selling points, the benefits, what would persuade them to back this project, how to present it. You draw on your experience, your knowledge, and you look at what others do in similar situations. You put together your package using your left-brain logical creativity. If you are unsuccessful, you make changes or try another financing source.

Thomas Edison used The Stubborn Tool when he invented the light bulb. He did over 10,000 experiments to find the right filament and gas. After 10,000 tries he was asked why he kept on after so many failures. Edison replied, "You don't understand. I have not failed over 10,000 time. I have found over 10,000 ways not to make a light bulb."

So working step by step, testing, changing, keeping on, until you get your result are the attributes of The Stubborn Tool. It's one of the most commonly used tools. During the process, which is often long, you will probably need to use other tools, to get your mind off in a different direction, if what you are doing is not working.

Ask What if...

The Explorer Tool

The purpose of this tool is to get you to ponder, to get you thinking on a grand scale. It's the dreamer's question. For Columbus it was "What if the earth is round and I could get to the riches of the East by sailing west?". For the Wright brothers it was "What if people could fly in a flying machine?". For Martin Luther King, Jr. it was "What if Americans, blacks and whites, were treated equally?".

"What-if" questions challenge us to think big. To jar us out of our routine mind-sets, to go beyond the known, into the what if it's possible. What if I tried this? When we ask "what if", the next step is how to. Then step-by-step work through how. Use logic, experiments, observations. If it does not work, make changes and try again. Now we are looking for new solutions, new ideas.

What if questions are similar to "why can't I" questions. But we tend to associate "why can't I" with whiney complaints (if they can land someone on the moon, why can't they make a computer that doesn't crash?). "What if" questions lift us out of that and get us to soar instead. And when we deal with negative thinking, "what if" questions are expressed as "why not". Whenever someone says "it can't be done", to get yourself (and maybe them) out of the old, routine thinking, and into creativity, reply "why not". Keep asking "why not" until you get into problem-solving.

So how do you construct "what if" questions? Look around you. Pick something. When you are reading the paper, or a book, choose a problem. Watch television. You will be overwhelmed by the selection of problems on that medium. Now what would you like to see? What annoyances do you want fixed? What dreams can you envision? Ask, "what if...?".

What if I could manufacture a home water production kit, to make each home self-sufficient for the expected future water shortage? What if I could manufacture water by distilling polluted or salt water, or collecting and purifying rain water? Distillation is a simple process. Moonshiners know that. What if I could buy hydrogen cylinders and manufacture water (H_2O) from the hydrogen and air (oxygen)?

What if I could manufacture a home medical kit for the diagnosis of the twenty most common serious illnesses? Diagnosis is as important as treatment. Just as we have a diagnostic hook-up for cars, what if I could develop a human equivalent?

What if I could develop a cheap, environmentally friendly, and easy to construct building material and design for housing?

What if I could grow food in large stacking containers or pallets so that the production on one acre of land could be multiplied by however many stacks I piled up? And since these containers are moveable, how can I devise a system to move them efficiently, to a safe haven in the event of frost, hurricanes, or floods? Or as a marketing tool, to place pallets of tomato plants in the supermarket, so customers could pick their own, fresh off the vine? Or daffodils in the florists shop, so customers could cut their own flowers?

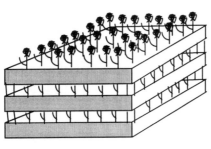

Stacking pallets.

What if I could fold my car up so it would take less space for parking?

What if my car ran on air?

What if my car fixed itself? What if my car was self-lubricating? Just as we have no-maintenance batteries, what if my car engine oiled itself, or did not need oil?

What if my car never needed insurance? I only need insurance because of accidents. What if my car was accident-proof?

What if my car never needed replacement? What if I could upgrade it like my computer? What if the parts could be plugged in, simply, like a light-bulb. I take out the old part (the engine), and pop in the new. No mechanic, no mess, no cost.

Now I am off, churning out all the petty annoyances I suffered from my car over the years. This question has jarred me out of my old thinking (I've got to get gas, I need an oil change, the insurance is due) and into different possibilities. I have created new ideas, which I can take to The Stubborn Tool or The Improvement Tools or some other tool to see what I end up with.

And the list goes on, because dreams are endless, only bounded by our beliefs and attitudes. And it's said if you can dream it, you can do it. So what dreams can you create with The Explorer Tool?

Take it apart.
Put it together
differently.

The Break Apart Tool

Take a question or problem apart and put it together in a different order. This will get your mind thinking in a new way. This tool works well for sequences; if you have a policy or operation you want to simplify, or action that you want done faster. What is the sequence for:

getting a loan?
applying for re-zoning?
obtaining a permit?
boarding an airplane?
assembling a car?
enrolling for a course?

List the sequence step-by-step. Then re-arrange the steps, put them together in a different order. Leave out a step. Do you remember taking a clock apart and when you put it back together, there was a spare part and it still worked? Changing the order of a sequence forces your mind into thinking differently. You are out of your rut. Now you can come up with something new. It forces you to see detail that you take for granted. This may spark a new association which will lead to a new idea.

This tool also works well if you have a picture in your mind. Take a part from that picture out and attach it somewhere else. The fact that it does not fit will jar your mind into a new direction. Picture a car. Take the wheels off and put them in the trunk. Now your mind is thinking how does the car move with no wheels or what good is it with no trunk space? Your mind is off thinking in a new direction. If your car had no wheels, how could it move? Would it need a propeller like an airplane, pulling it just above the ground? Or a jet engine. If cars are steam-lined and designed like an airplane wing, could you get them to fly just above the road? Or would it use

air propulsion like a hover-craft, lifting it off the
ground? What about rails or a reverse electro-
magnetic force, pushing the car off the ground?
Instead of wheels, you could use a caterpillar
system like a snowmobile. Maybe you could use
roller-bearings. What would reduce friction? Do
you want more surface contact or less? What
would give a smoother ride? What's wrong with
tires? Maybe instead of four tires, you could have
many thin tires, bicycle-thin. If you had many
thin tires, tires small enough to fit under the car,
would this give you a smoother ride? And if a tire
went flat, it would not matter, because there are
several others to take up the slack. So the change
in the picture has sent your mind travelling down
a different road, asking questions you would not
normally think of, looking at new possibilities. It
has given you a different perspective.

Chapter Eight

The
Left-Brain
Lateral
Tools

To be creative,

you must

break out

of old patterns

of thinking

and replace them

with new.

The Left-Brain Lateral Tools

Lateral thinking starts out like logical thinking, step-by-step.   Then something triggers our thoughts in another direction, and from there we proceed step-by-step.

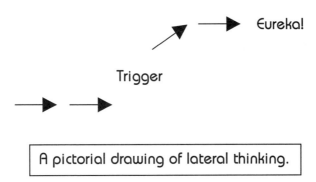

| A pictorial drawing of lateral thinking. |

The lateral tools inspire that something which triggers our thoughts in another direction.   The lateral tools are the triggers.   There are three of them:

1. The Change Tool
2. The Impossible Tool
3. The Contrary Tool

Change a Characteristic.

bigger/smaller

faster/slower

more/fewer

stronger/weaker

harder/easier

expensive/free

Add something on.
Take something off.

The Change Tool

The Change Tool is the most basic. You simply change a characteristic of your problem or question. Now you are looking at your problem in a new light, from a different angle. The process is to list all the characteristics of your problem. Now pick a characteristic and change it. You can add something on or take something off. Add a picture or draw your problem as a picture. Put in a sound or change a sound or make it silent. Change the appeal (to a different group).

Change a characteristic: take something off.

You can make it bigger or smaller. Change the taste: make it sweet, sour, salty, or tasteless. Change the texture, softness, hardness, or pattern. Change or add a smell: fragrant, musk, light, strong, apple pie, cinnamon.

Faster or slower	Heavier or lighter
More expensive or cheaper	Hotter or colder
Artificial or real	Funny or serious
On top or underneath	Old or new
Light or dark	Complex or simple
Informal or formal	Higher or lower
Grand or quaint	Fly or walk
And the list goes on.	

The person who developed paper back books used The Change Tool—changing the hardcover to paper. Aluminum bats meant a change in the characteristic from wood to metal.

102 Creating Ideas
Alice Steinbart

Supermarkets were a change in the characteristic of size.

So let's try this tool:

How can I speed up grocery store line-ups?

List the characteristics:
groceries are purchased at a store
most products have bar codes
people line up at cashiers
people put groceries into shopping carts
cashiers ring up the sales
people pay with cash, cheques, credit or
    debit cards

Now let's pick one of these characteristics and change it:

people line up at cashiers.

Change that to there are no cashiers and no line ups.

If there are no cashiers, then how do you ring up the sales? What if every person acts as the cashier and has a pen scanner attached to the shopping cart? They scan in the product as they buy it, and it is automatically charged to their account or debit card. Or if it is a cash sale or by cheque, then a running total is printed out, and cash is paid to a receiver at the exit who gives change or takes the cheque, without having to ring in the products. The receiver also collects the credit or debit slip. The bar code label is security sensitive so that if a product has not been scanned in, a security warning goes off as the customer leaves the store. A product that does not have a bar code, such as produce, can have one placed on it, either by a produce clerk or an automatic bar coder, after the customer has picked, bagged, weighed, and labeled it. If a customer scans in a product and then decides she does not want it, she can go to a return counter and scan in the return and leave the product there, or the scanner attached to the shopping cart could have that feature, which would at the same time re-sensitize the security feature on the bar code.

Normally the question of how to speed up grocery sales (or any type of sales) would produce answers like hire more cashiers, have a single line so the next person goes to the next available cashier, have more express lanes, have better bar coding, have better trained cashiers. The Change Tool forces your thinking out of this traditional pattern. Your mind, your viewpoint is now somewhere else, producing new, creative ideas. Now you take the ideas to The Improvement Tools to see if you can make them work.

What cannot be done?
Why not?
Now do it.

The Impossible Tool

"It can't be done." Teeth-gnashing words. Words not fit to be spoken by a creative. This tool deliberately looks for things that supposedly cannot be done. The purpose of The Impossible Tool is to get you looking for possibilities. What can't be done? Why not? Now do it. It forces you to make connections and associations, so you will come up with ideas you would never have thought of otherwise. It's useful for dealing with negative thinkers.

The impossible idea you come up with may truly be impossible in that form. But the idea is a trigger, leading you to another idea. It may be that a modification of the impossibility will make it possible.

Let's try an example. You can't have your cake and eat it too. You can't have your money and give it away.

Why not? Now do it.

Why can't you have your money and someone else also have it? What if you want to give it to your children, but you also want to keep it? If you gave it to them and they lent it back to you, then you could pay them interest so they will have the income. They also know they will eventually have the principal amount, as you will pay it back. You may be able to declare the interest you pay as tax deductible. This may even work better with a charitable donation. You want to give to your favourite charity, but you still need your money. You give the charity the gift and they lend it back to you. You pay them interest and you get a tax deduction for the charitable donation. You may also get a tax deduction on the interest you pay on the loan. That way you have your money and the charity has your money and you also have a tax deduction. Now you need to check to find out if the tax department will allow such a deduction.

What about another example? What cannot be done with walkways?

They can't be rolled up and moved.
They can't sing.
They can't be eaten.
They can't do arithmetic.
They can't juggle.

Why not? Now do it.

Why can't footpaths be rolled up and moved. Artificial turf can be. Think of the wear and tear on it: football players clashing, marching bands parading, horses galloping, cars driving around. It gets a real work-out. So what material could be used to make a sidewalk that is strong, yet flexible enough to be rolled up and moved. What weave and density would work? What type of underlay could you use that would be acceptable after the walk was taken away? What material could you use so you would not need an underlay?

And why can't footpaths sing? And if not sing, then at least talk, to give directions. Or for advertisements. If not done vocally, then what if ads were written on the footpaths? What if the sound does not come from the path itself, but from the fence or edging or posts along the path? What if the sound was a beat for joggers or cyclists to keep pace? Would that make the path more attractive to joggers or cyclists? What effect does sound have on the performance or the enjoyment of a jogger or cyclist or a cross-country skier or anyone in a race? What if the sound was white noise to drown out the city background? What if it was not sound, but noise reducers? What catches sound without destroying the ambience?

Look at all the possibilities you have spun. You can take any of them and turn to The Improvement Tools to see what ideas you can make workable. The Impossible Tool has got you to look at your question from a new angle and see it in a different light. This is the creative process.

Mismatch.

How are these different?

The Contrary Tool

This tool gets you to focus on differences and find connections you would not normally make. Connections are like associations; one leads to another, and you will end up someplace you never thought of before. Most people are matchers, they find similarities. Looking for dissimilarities gets you thinking in a new direction. If you are normally a mis-matcher, this tool will not make much difference to you.

This is the tool you use when someone says "you can't compare apples to oranges". Well, yes you can. They are both fruits. You can compare them on vitamin value, the ease of growing, the profitability of growing one compared to the other, the cost to the consumer. You can compare them on related products—apple juice to orange juice. You can find similarities, even with supposedly different things. So anytime someone says "that does not apply to us", or "it's not the same" or "our situation is different", this tool forces you out of that mind-set.

Looking for differences has a value. It will get your mind thinking in a new direction, to come up with other ideas. If you are an airline looking for greater profitability, what ideas could you create by looking for the differences between air travel and cars?

> cars are more restricted because they are limited to roads
>
> planes are more versatile when in the air as they can fly anywhere
>
> planes are more restricted on the ground, to airports
>
> cars are cheaper
>
> planes are faster
>
> flying requires more skill than driving

planes can take small or large groups, cars
    can only take individuals or small
    groups
cars are more dangerous, but planes are
    perceived as more dangerous
individuals are more likely to own a car
    than a plane
planes cover greater distances, faster

This sets you to thinking about the
limitations of both. Planes are almost unlimited
when flying and limited to airports when on the
ground. Cars are limited to roads. Then you
start to wonder why just look at planes and cars,
why not all forms of travel: trains, buses, boats?

Trains are limited to the rail lines. But
they have an advantage as they have a corridor, a
land strip that is for their use only. They can also
go faster and haul more than cars. On the other
hand, they are expensive. Then the thought
comes, what if you take the best of all the modes
of travel? The speed of planes, the bulk-carrying
of trains, and the cheapness of cars and the
control you feel having your own car. So now if
you have a jet powered car (from plane
technology) using the train corridors, you could
have stacking rails consisting of the railbed for
trains, and a second and third level above for high
speed cars, with one level for each direction.
People could drive their cars onto a single rail car,
have their car strapped down and the rail car set
off on the rail corridor at airplane speed. At the
destination, the individual in their car drives off.

Now these are grand ideas, so in the
interim are there some ideas I can take and use?
First, there is the idea of exploring cooperation
between different methods of travel. How can
airlines, railways, and car manufacturers work
together for their mutual benefit instead of seeing
each other as competitors? They are all offering

travel. What can they offer each other? Just as car rental agencies in airports have a symbiotic relationship with airlines.

Second, one of the ideas that twigged is cars are popular, in part because of the control the owner has. It's my car. I decide when and where I go. I am in control. But when I fly or go by bus or train, I have to use their route, their schedule, and their equipment. How can planes, trains, and buses make the traveler feel more in control, as if they were in their own car? Perception is important. After all, cars are more dangerous than planes, but people perceive planes as more dangerous. In any event, using The Contrary Tool has pointed your thinking in a direction you would not have taken without it. You can continue to explore some of the ideas generated to see what else comes up, or you can go to The Improvement Tools to see how you can make your ideas work.

"One of our mistakes
is insisting
a thing is impossible
because
we cannot accomplish it."
Cicero

Chapter Nine

The
Borrowing
Tools

The Borrowing Tools

Borrowing is one of the easiest ways of creating something new. If you look around, you will see so many examples. Was the idea for above-ground pools borrowed from seeing children's wading pools? The car came from putting together carriages and the gas engine. The first cars were sometimes called "horseless carriages". Did comedy clubs come from the idea of night clubs? The zip lock is based on the tongue and grove in carpentry. Did the person who developed reclining seats see a bed and think "wouldn't it be nice to have a chair that stretched out into a bed"? Traffic signals came from someone borrowing the idea of lights to put on traffic signs.

The Borrowing Tools are useful for business people looking for more business. What can you combine with your business to make you stand out in your field, or better still to make your business more attractive to customers? We all know the usual answers—longer hours, better service, offer something free or reduce the price. The Borrowing Tools can get you to move beyond the mundane solutions to that dynamic innovation that moves you ahead.

The possibilities of combining ideas or borrowing ideas increases as we get more ideas and more products. This field is expanding. We are just beginning to mine the potential that The Borrowing Tools give us.

There are six Borrowing Tools:
1. The Combining Tool
2. The Booty Tool
3. The Mind Jar Tool
4. The Role-playing Tool
5. The Opinion Tool
6. The Hawk-eyes Tool

Combine

the first two things

you see.

The Combining Tool

The Combining Tool tells you to put together things that you would never have thought of associating. Now you have forced your mind into looking at something new. You are making connections you would not normally make. Sometimes we think of putting together two things to come up with something new; a phone and a tape recorder to get the answering machine or a printer, scanner, fax, copier to get the multi-function machine. This tool does not allow you to select what you want to combine, but tells to pick two things at random. Then you are forced to work with making something useful from this combination. It may not work at first, but it will trigger new ideas as you improvise a solution. Ultimately, you will end up with ideas you would not have created without this forced fit.

Look around you. Pick the first two things you see. The carpet and ceiling lights. Now combine them.

You get lighting from the floor—a lit carpet.

The carpet is translucent; you can see through it.

The carpet is made of plastic or glass, like the light fixtures.

The ceiling has carpeting on it.

The lights are made of fabric.

You cannot see the lights because the carpets cover them.

Now you pick one and see what you can do with it. The carpet is translucent. Or what if it's clear? This would be an advantage if you had a hardwood floor. Then you could get the beauty of the wood but keep it protected. A carpet is softer to walk on and makes the room quieter. If you did not have a hard wood floor, but tile or vinyl, you get the benefits of a carpet, soft, quiet. Maybe you could lay something on the floor, like paper or glass, that you could not normally walk on, but now could, as the clear carpet protected it. What advantage would a paper or glass floor give you? Stained glass is beautiful. Suppose you had a stained glass floor, and it was lit? Or paper— maybe you could have beautiful paintings on the floor? After all we have paintings on the ceiling— Michelangelo painted the Sistine Chapel. What effect would a painted floor have on a room? Would it make it more grand, more beautiful, more luxurious? Even if you did not have a clear carpet to cover it, but simply painted murals on the floor, what would that do to a room? We paint murals on the outside of buildings and long walls, so why not on floors? And if you wanted to protect it, we have clear coatings to do that.

So The Combining Tool has got you out of your usual pattern of thinking, to create new ideas. The Combining Tool is useful when you want to find other uses. Finding other uses is a valuable marketing and sales tool. You have a product you want to sell. If you think of other uses for that product, you will increase your sales. So you start combining your product with everything you see or can think of. Some combinations will not work, but may spark ideas that will. Other combinations may work with some changes. The more uses you can create, the more you will increase your sales. The Combining Tool is valuable.

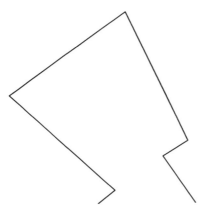

There is always

another idea.

Take an idea
from another field.

The Booty Tool

Take an idea from somewhere else and use it to get you thinking about how it could work in your field. People in other fields have problems similar to yours. What ideas did they use to solve their problems? Can you modify these ideas to fit your needs? If a solution works somewhere else, why not for you?

This tool differs from The Combining Tool. The Combining Tool tells you to take the first two things you see and put them together. The Booty Tool gets you to be selective about what you pick. You do not join the first things you see, but rather you look for successful ideas in other fields and apply them. If you wanted to increase your sales, you could ask "how can I increase my sales", or you could ask "how has the fastest growing company last year done it?"

Are the big box retail stores successful at marketing? How do they do it and what can you learn from them? Is research and development in the medical field successful?   Then what techniques do they use that you can apply or modify? Is customer satisfaction high in fast food restaurants? Can you copy it? Or can you reverse it? If someone is unsuccessful, then what can you learn from their mistakes?

One of the most visible examples of the use of The Booty Tool is the radio. How many things have been joined to the radio to produce new products? The radio has been combined with the tape recorder. Headphones were added. We have the clock radio, which can also be used as an alarm. The car radio was combined with the tape deck.   Radio has been hooked to some phone systems, so you hear the radio while you wait on hold.   Or the radio is hooked into the public address system, maybe in your dentist's office. The radio is a versatile joiner.

The S.O.S. scouring pads are a simple example of combining. In 1917, Edwin Cox was trying to sell aluminum cookware door-to-door. Aluminum pots were new and housewives were not receptive to a demonstration. so he came up with the idea of offering something free if they would agree to a demonstration. Then he needed to get creative on what to offer. He knew baked on food was a problem and he used The Booty Tool to come up with the idea of combining abrasive steel wool with soap. He soaked the steel wool in soap, dried it, soaked it again and again until he had his scouring pad. It worked. The pads were so successful, he made more money selling them than cookware. So he changed directions and stopped selling cookware and started manufacturing his pads.

If you think of all the ideas and products we have, then the possibilities of mixing and matching them are endless, especially when we keep developing new ideas and products, which themselves become new possibilities to join with existing products or ideas.

"Ideas are
a dime a dozen.
People who put
them into action
are priceless."
                    Anonymous

The Mind Jar Tool

This tool is pure association which gets you looking at your problem from a fresh angle. Pick a noun or verb at random and apply it to your question or problem. You will now have associations you would never otherwise have made. These associations will eventually spark new ideas.

Let's try it. I am a phone company looking to sign up more long-distance subscribers. I decide to pick the ingredient of clown from my Mind Jar. When I think of clown, I think:

dressing up in funny clothes
entertainment
children
happy
big feet

I pick one—entertainment. What entertainment could a long distance time seller provide to get more subscribers? Two possibilities come to mind: first, entertainment as a reward for subscribing, either by funny ads or a contest with an entertaining prize; and second, getting entertainment after subscribing. The technology exists to have a video camera set up with your phone so you can see who you are talking to. Could this be adapted so a long distance subscriber could dial up and pick a video to watch or plug into a favourite out of area radio station, or pick which music or talk show to listen to? And since they might not want to tie up their phone while watching or listening, they might buy a second line, or at least a call-waiting feature. So now associating clown with long distance phone subscribers has forced my thinking ideas other than the usual lower price, discounts, and specials.

Where do you get a noun or verb at random?   You create a Mind Jar.   You can physically use a jar, box, or notebook.   Write down a selection of words, some nouns, some action verbs.   Keep them handy and when you want an ingredient from your Mind Jar, pick one. The ingredients need to be diverse and rich in associations.   Thus   you   will   have   more associations from a computer than a can opener. A can opener might get you to think of kitchens, cans, and cutting.   But computers will prompt work, games, fun, challenge, crashes, computer illiterate, anxiety, Windows, Apple, programs, amazing, monitor, mouse, mouse pad, and many more. It is the better ingredient in your Mind Jar.

If you do not have your Mind Jar with you, the yellow pages of a phone book, or a dictionary, or any other book will work.   Simply open the book and point.   There's your word.   If these books are not available, then pick anything from your surroundings.

The Mind Jar differs from The Combining Tool because you have purposely selected the ingredients to put in your Mind Jar.   And you have selected the ingredients based on the myriad of associations they call up for you.

A few examples are included on the following pages. You can add your own; whatever stimulates new ideas for you.

Some Mind Jar Ingredients.

How is this like
singing?

How is this like
a computer?

How is this like
a credit card?

How is this like a clown?

How is this like farming?

How is this like a photocopier?

How is this like stress?

How is this like winning a contest?

How is this like time?

How would
another person do it?

Tinker  Tailor
Soldier Sailor
Rich Poor
Beggar Thief
Doctor Lawyer
Merchant Chief

The Role-Playing Tool

The Role-playing Tool gets us to look at our problem from another perspective. People in the same occupations or roles often have similar outlooks and attributes. We assume advertising agents have certain characteristics in common, which differ from the characteristics of a teacher, which in turn differ from the characteristics of a mechanic. So if an advertising agent is faced with the same problem as a teacher and a mechanic, each would, because of their characteristics, approach the question differently. If you asked how can you improve television, the answers you would get from an advertising agent would focus around money, or television ads selling more products, or improving the ads, or increasing the watch rate of ads. A teacher would look at better programming or even less programming. A mechanic would see the technological aspects, such as what makes the television give a better picture or sound, how could it be more easily repaired and made more convenient to use.

To use this tool, at random, pick an occupation, either by looking around you, or thinking of your family's or friends' occupations, or opening the yellow pages of the phone book and picking the first occupation you see. Then pretend that is your occupation. Now how does the problem look? Are you looking at it in a different light? How would a person in that occupation solve it? The purpose here is to get you thinking in a new way, so that you can come up with fresh ideas.

Get others' opinions.

The Opinion Tool

Everyone is unique.

No two people think alike.

These realities make The Opinion Tool useful. We all have our own separate experiences and therefore will make dissimilar associations. When I look at a problem or have a question, I am going to handle it differently from you. But if I get suggestions, ideas, or advice from you, that may change my approach. Now I am thinking something else. I am looking at it from a new angle.

The Opinion Tool differs from The Role-playing Tool as it is based on individual's ideas and not on occupational similarities. People are more than their occupations. They have viewpoints, personalities, and attributes in addition to their occupational characteristics.

If you are the owner of a shopping center concerned about the empty retail spaces and you asked your tenants for their ideas, you would get some standard answers—lower the rent, give more benefits, give a bonus of free rent, advertise for tenants. But you may well get some unique answers, that spark your thinking in another direction. Suggestions might include put in a customer rest area with carpeting, soft chairs, and easy lighting, install information on the tenants, along with a map of the mall, and allow tenants to put in displays of their goods. Put in a play area for children. Put in a demonstration area from educational to entertaining, such as clowns, school choirs, bands, and fashion shows. Ask hobbyists, social groups, or crafters to put on a workshop or show. Be the first to show off new products or fads. For example, if none of the tenants sell televisions, have a company in to demonstrate new high resolution televisions. Be innovative in looking for new tenants, such as setting up a browsing area for catalogues of products not sold by your tenants, with telephones for people to phone in an order. Arrange with catalogue sellers to have a percentage paid to the mall. And who knows what other ideas your tenants can think of? It is in their interest to keep a busy mall and get people in. You might be able to arrange to have them contribute to the cost as part of the common elements.

In any event, your mind is now off in a different direction and you are coming up with new ideas, which you can take to The Improvement Tools to see if they work.

**Ask ten
different
people for a
solution
and you will
probably get
ten different
answers.**

Pay attention.

The Hawk-eyes Tool

When you pay attention, you notice things you would otherwise pass by. When you buy a new car, suddenly you see that particular colour or style or model everywhere. If you are looking for a new computer, immediately there are so many ads or sales for computers. They were always there, but you never noticed. When you pay attention, you will see more. You are now making connections and associations which will lead to new ideas.

The Hawk-eyes Tool also tells you to look at your problem more closely. What is actually going on here? What are you overlooking? Let's try an example. What would you do if your car was stuck in the snow (or mud), and you had no shovel, no phone, no help, and no houses nearby? This forces you to pay attention to what you do have—in your car or around you. One set of answers focuses on getting out—using the car floor mats as traction, or the hub caps as make-shift shovels, or finding things in your trunk to use as tools or traction. Maybe you have rope and something you can fashion into a pulley to make a winch. Another set of answers focuses on how you can get help—make a sign, a bonfire, or a flag. Still a third set of answers might look at walking out—checking a map, climbing a high point to find out where you are, how far do you have to go, do you have food, water, walking boots, warmth, time?

So you can pay attention to:

1. what is out there—ideas you can apply from other places;

2. the creativity process, what is going on with your problem or your way of thinking about it. Maybe you need to go back to The Detective Tool and ask different questions. Or maybe go

back to The Flip Tool and ask your question differently.   Or maybe to The Rebel Tool and check your beliefs and expectations.   Are they limiting your creativity?;

3. the details of your problem.

Paying attention gets you to see more and into thinking along alternate lines. What you look at makes a difference. The solution depends on what you are looking for. A different focus will produce a different result. Pyrex cooking ware proves this. Heat-tempered glass was invented in the 1800's, but it was used only in industry. No one thought to use it for cooking until 1915 when one of the workers at Corning Glass came up with the idea. And Pyrex became a mainstay of the company.

So if you want a creative idea, pay attention. Shift your focus.

Chapter Ten

The
Improvement
Tools

Everything
can be changed
or improved.

The Improvement Tools

This set of tools is the final step, the refinement stage of the creativity process. The Japanese have a term, kaizen, meaning constant and never ending improvement. Improvement puts you in the lead. Improving what you just sold your customer will bring you another sale to that customer. You buy a car. Now you want to move up to the next model with more options. You buy a computer. Now you want a faster one. You buy a television. Now you want a bigger screen or better resolution.

Everything can be improved, even if it's just presenting it in a new way or combining it with something else. When you improve something, you have created a new and better idea or product. Think of the changes we have made to cars since the old Model T, to airplanes since the Kittyhawk, and to fax machines since the first model. Improving an existing idea is a common form of creativity.

There are four Improvement Tools:
1. The Valuable Tool
2. The Garbage Tool
3. The Check-up Tool
4. The Stretch Tool

Everything has
something of value.
Find it.

The Valuable Tool

The Valuable Tool jars you out of negative judgement into a new approach of finding what works. It forces your thinking and creativity into a new direction. It is one of the most important tools for creativity. Our society teaches us to see the negative, to see what's wrong. It is difficult to get out of this thinking, into problem-solving. The Valuable Tool is your reminder to concentrate on problem-solving.

This is the tool to use when you meet opposition, when people find fault. You rarely get a perfect idea, requiring no changes or work. Most of your solutions are half-formed. They solve one problem, but create others. They do not mesh perfectly with your needs and require modifications. The Valuable Tool focuses you on what is useful about the idea, on what does work, so that you can keep this uppermost and not abandon this good idea, as you work out the kinks.

The early computers were enormous—the size of a house. Data was entered by rectangular cards with holes punched in them. Sometimes our bills came in the form of these rectangular cards and we were told "do not spindle, fold, or mutilate" because then they could not be fed into the computer. There were many flaws in these early computers. Even now we have problems. Yet they are still valuable.

When television became popular in the 1950's, it had many limitations. It was black and white. We were always fiddling with the sharpness and contrast buttons, trying to get a better picture, or adjusting the rabbit ears. Sometimes the rabbit ears ended up in some strange places in our living rooms. Programming was only on at night. Most of the time we had test pattern. And there was only one channel. Early opponents believed television, because of these and other drawbacks, would never be popular. This was just another idea that would end up on the scrap heap.

To use this tool, take an idea you have just created that does not work. Now what has to be changed and how do you do it? It may be you will use The Stubborn Tool to see if it works. If it does not, then try something else. Or maybe the value in this idea is that it sparks another, better idea.

A modern example of an idea that needs The Valuable Tool is air bags for people. People who are unsteady on their feet, who rely on canes or walkers, in-line skaters, beginning roller skaters or ice skaters or skiers, or bike riders, could all use air bags, on their knees, elbows, and heads.   Slim-fitting, non-obtrusive, maybe worn under clothes, never noticed until or unless there is the impact of a fall.   Then the air-bag would inflate and protect. Instead of a helmet, maybe a deflated air bag could be designed into a hat. In fact, maybe it is possible to use this technology for bullet-proof vests, making them lighter and easier to conceal. Of course, there are any number of bugs that would have to be worked out.   The Valuable Tool keeps you focused on preserving the idea and not abandoning it because it needs work.

If you are good at spotting what is wrong, then this tool will help you change your focus to spotting what can work.

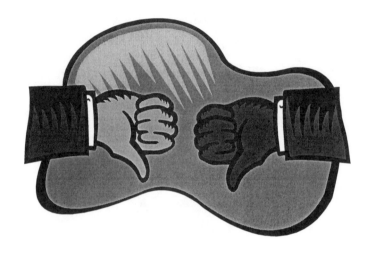

Every idea
has something that
makes it less valuable.
Change it.

The Garbage Tool

This tool is meant to be used on existing ideas, existing products. Very few of the things around us are in the same form as when they were first conceived. Almost everything you see around you has been improved in some way. The telephone invented by Alexander Graham Bell was so basic in its simplicity, that it almost seems closer to the two tin cans connected by a taunt string we played with as kids than to the modern telephone.

Money-making ideas come from looking for those things that do not work well in existing products. Once you spot the weakness, then you have an opportunity. You can fix this problem. If the existing product is making money, then an improved version will make money. The Garbage Tool gives your mind carte blanche to find faults. Then reins it in and tells it to fix them. This gives you a fresh perspective, from complaining to solving. New directions give new ideas.

So how do you spot what can be improved in an existing idea? Just look for what annoys you or what can go wrong with something. The Internet comes to mind. It has been much touted, but when you search for something on it, you get 100 entries, and most of them have nothing to do with what you are looking for. Some people may have the time or interest to look through these sites. You don't want to. Also you need to know how reliable this information is.

Up to now, the solution has been to improve the search engines or educate people how to describe their sites so that search engines can do a better job. What if you looked for a different method—developing an Information Center instead of a search engine? You could create data bases and consolidate data bases. You could

check the information.   You could provide full
service or self-service.   Full-service means your
customer tells you what they want and you find
the information, summarize it, and complete a
question and answer.   Self-service allows the
customer to search the data base themselves,
perhaps with some direction from you.

Creating an Information Center is a major
task, like writing the first dictionary or the first
encyclopedia. But we are in the Information Age
and easy, reliable access to information is
valuable.

So you have produced a new idea using The
Garbage Tool.

Everyone

is creative.

**Every idea
can be improved.
How?**

The Check-up Tool

The Check-up Tool is meant to be used on existing ideas, existing products. It differs from The Valuable Tool, which is for new ideas, and from The Garbage Tool, which looks at what does not work in an existing idea. The Check-up Tool accepts that everything is working fine, and looks for what can make it better.

There are very few things which cannot, in some way, be made better. This tool gets you to look for what needs fixing. Look around you. Most of what you see has been improved over time. The chair you sit on may be cushioned, have rollers on it, be ergonomically designed, tilt, vibrate, extend. The first chairs were hard, rigid, and immovable. Your photocopier collates, enlarges, reduces, is faster, and can print in colour, all refinements on the first models. Your car has air-conditioning, a great sound system, a tape deck, seat belts, movable seats, and many other developments from the early cars. What other improvements can you see around you?

The process is to ask "What would make this better?" or "What can I do to make this better?". You can also find improvement when you say "they should...". They should make a printer that never needs ink. They should make a vacuum that never needs a bag replacement. They should make a drain that never clogs.

You are surrounded by things that could be made better. The Check-up Tool gets you to notice them.

12...

**Everything
has another use.
Find
twelve more uses.**

The Stretch Tool

One of the more common creativity tools is to find more uses for what we already have, to use something in a new way.   Most of what we have can be used for something else. Think of all the places where hinges are used. If you look around, I bet you will spot something which has a hinge. Not only on doors of all kinds, from cupboards to rooms to storage doors, but also on double or triple picture frames, some cell phones, many things that fold, such as folding chairs, tables, doors, fold-up beds, collapsible strollers, cribs, and highchairs.   No doubt there are more places where we could use hinges.

Usually when we are looking for a solution, we come up with traditional, usual, even the worn out, ineffective ideas first. The Stretch Tool gets you to move beyond that to creative new ideas. So after you have listed all the usual ideas, now find 12 more.   "Oh, but I exhausted all the possibilities," you say. No, there are always more ideas. Use another tool to get your mind off in another direction. The more ideas you come up with, the more likely one will be that powerful idea that is just right. And although this Tool tells you to find 12 more uses, 12 is only a figure. You will do better if you find 15 more, or 20, or 100. There should never be a number limit, only a time limit;   meaning I only want to spend this much time creating ideas, not "I need only create 12 ideas".

To use The Stretch Tool, simply list as many other uses as come to mind.   Go for at least a dozen new uses. Often one use will spark an idea for another. Also looking around you will give new possibilities.   Don't worry if, as you produce them, some don't make sense.   Write them down, as they are part of the connection to the next idea, which may prove to be good.

So what are a dozen more uses for credit cards:

1. screwdriver (using the edge as a slot screwdriver)
2. knife (sharpen the edge for cutting)
3. medical history
4. i.d.
5. driver's licence
6. cash card, debit card, and credit card combined
7. banking card
8. all cards (whatever you have in your wallet—calling card, library card, long distance card, video store card)
9. calculator
10. radio
11. clock
12. ruler

Some of the ideas may be workable such as combining more cards or even all cards onto the credit card, so you carry only a few or even one. So the ideas from numbers 3 to 8, sparked from one idea to another. Once you started thinking about putting medical history on the card, you proceeded to thinking of other things to put on the card, until you eventually suggested everything.

You began the list looking for uses that would be out of the ordinary for credit cards and thus in numbers 1 and 2, got screwdriver and knife. These may not be useful ideas, except in emergencies when you needed to improvise.

In ideas 9 to 12, you used The Combining Tool, combining a radio, clock, calculator and ruler to the credit card. Our miniaturization technology may not be far enough advanced to accomplish this, but if technology catches up, having a calculator as part of your credit card would be a useful idea.

So now just listing a dozen more uses, you have a couple of new ideas you might be able to work with. The more ideas you list, the more possibilities you will come up with.

If none of the ideas you produced appeal to you, go back and find 12 more uses. If you feel you cannot think of more, pick another tool to spark you creativity. Maybe The Mind Jar, with a new association, will get your thinking going in another direction, to give you different ideas.

This book
gives you the tools
to be creative at will.
It is up to you
what you do with them.
Some people
leave their tools
out in the rain
to get rusty.
Others use their tools
to build themselves
a mansion.
What will you do with yours?

Chapter Eleven

Conclusion

There is no
guarantee
your idea
will be accepted.
But I can guarantee
you will get
plenty of ideas.

Brainstorming

So why has brainstorming not been included as one of the tools? After all up to now, if anyone wanted to come up with a creative idea, they would probably be told "try brainstorming". Brainstorming is not a tool, but a process. It sets up an environment that encourages creativity. And that's important.   Once you have the environment, you will spontaneously use the tools. Participants do it without realizing.   Someone calls out an idea. This sparks an association in another person's mind, which leads to another idea.   They yell it out, sparking another suggestion. It's all based on connections and now you are getting others' associations, which of course will be different from your own. So this causes your thinking to go off in a new direction, producing new ideas.

There are some rules on how it's done:

1. The group should be a certain size, five to seven people are best. If it's too small, you will not get as many ideas. If it's too large it may be overwhelming and too cumbersome.

2. There must be no judgement or criticism. Saying an idea will not work, will shut down creativity. Judgement or evaluation comes after the session, not during.

3. The ideas must be recorded. Either someone writes them down or the session is taped, so later the ideas can be gathered.

In addition to these rules, there are guidelines:

1. The goal should be many ideas, not necessarily good ideas, because if you look for good ideas at this stage, you will be getting into judgement. Also, since one idea sparks another, many ideas will spark many more. And of course,

the more ideas you have, the more likely that you will have some gems.

2. Adding onto an idea, changing it in some way, or combining it with another are good techniques.

3. The Silly Tool is an excellent way to start a brainstorming session. It gets the lightness and humour going, and silences the critic.

4. Have a leader or facilitator responsible for calling the session, getting a note-taker, presenting the problem or question, asking for the first idea, ending the session, and later calling the evaluation session.

5. Have an evaluation session a day or two later. Waiting allows the ideas to settle and incubate. The purpose of evaluation is to find which ideas can work, with the use of The Improvement Tools, if necessary.

Evaluation

After you produce your ideas, you will need to evaluate or judge them. Think of evaluation as harvesting. When the farmer harvests, the crop, or parts of the crop, may be Grade A. Some crops may be lower grades. All the grades are used, even if only for animal feed or compost. The only difference is the lower grades sell for less.

Grade your ideas. Grade A are workable ideas. Lower grades are still useable. Some ideas may be useful as triggers for other ideas, or for combining with alternate ideas to produce something new. Or you may put your idea aside for later, perhaps for technology to catch up. Or maybe you do not need that idea now. It was not what you were looking for. So like canning or preserving, you put the idea into storage, for later use. Or maybe someone else can use your idea.

Keep all your ideas, even if they seem

unworkable. Maybe someday you will use one of them or they may inspire new ideas. Ideas should be treated like books. They are precious and not to be thrown away. If you do not want them, then like books, give them to someone who does.

Also keep a file of your uncompleted ideas—works in progress. They will be a source for you. Either you will go back and complete them, when you are ready, or they will trigger new ideas for you.

All your ideas have a value, and that is the starting point for your evaluation.

Duplicate Ideas

How many times have you come up with an idea, did not do anything about it, and then later saw someone else had put it into effect, and was making money on it. It is common for people to separately come up with the same or similar ideas, at about the same time.

The wheelbarrow is an example of this. It developed independently in China and in Europe.

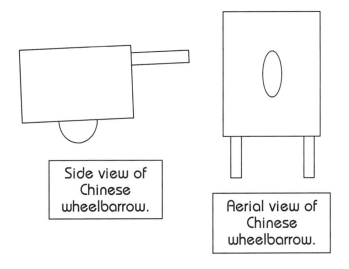

Side view of
Chinese
wheelbarrow.

Aerial view of
Chinese
wheelbarrow.

About 200 A.D., it was modified from the two-wheeled hand-cart used by farmers in China. The two-wheeled cart was too wide for some narrow tracks so an enterprising Chinese put one wheel in the center of the cart, balanced between the right and left sides and the front and back. There were no legs to rest on, but there were handles for maneuvering. About 1000 years later, Europeans devised a wheelbarrow, but they put the wheel at the front and the first barrow had no legs to rest on, although they did have handles to maneuver. Because the European wheelbarrow had the wheel at the front, the worker had to support part of the weight, as well as maneuver the barrow. The Chinese version was balanced, so the worker did not need to hold up any weight, simply maneuver. Similar ideas developing separately, and interestingly the less technologically efficient barrow, the European barrow, has still not been replaced in Western society by the Chinese barrow.

So you will come up with ideas that other have had, or someone will duplicate your idea. The key issue is not so much who developed it first, but who is the better marketer.

Type of Tool

Everyone who created an idea, got to their creativity by using one of the tools in this book. They probably did not recognize they were using the tool. You too may be creative without being aware of using the tools.

Some tools lend themselves to certain types of questions. For example, The Valuable Tool is used when you might be inclined to discard an idea. It works well with The Silly Tool. You come up with an unworkable idea, then use The Valuable Tool to find out what is worthwhile about the idea.   However, it would not work with an existing idea such as closets for storage, as the idea is already practical.   What might work instead is The Check-up Tool—how can you improve your closets?   Or perhaps The Stretch Tool, find 12 more uses for a closet (assuming, of course, you have empty closets).

The person who came up with the water-bed may have used The Booty Tool—putting together the ideas of bed and how good it felt floating on water.   Or maybe they used The Detective Tool.   What would be softer than a pillow? What would take the shape of a body, but not lump up like feathers?

If you wanted to increase your business, The Borrowing Tools and The Stretch Tool are useful. If you get stuck, try The Start-up Tools, The Preparation Tools, or The Incubation Tool. The Improvement Tools are for fixing a product or idea.

When you start creating, you do not know where you will end up. You have no control over that.   But you do control where you are going to start. You control what question you will ask and how you will word it. You control which tool you will use. Each tool gives a slant to your thinking. If you choose The Rebel Tool, you will go in a different direction than if you chose The Booty Tool. So you never know where you will end up or what ideas you will produce.

Each tool will jog different associations. So if you pick one tool it will stimulate one idea, but a different tool will spark another idea. How do you know which tool is best? Experiment. If one tool is not comfortable or productive, try another. For example, you are a financial planner and you want to get more clients.   I recommend The Combining Tool or The Booty Tool. What else can you do or combine with your services, that would attract clients?   Can you borrow an idea from another field?

The tools in this book are an organizing system. It may not be organized in the right way for you. So find different words, or pictures, use the tools in a different way, or find different tools. Do what works for you.

That's Silly

Yes,   everything   starts   off   as   silly, impractical, too expensive, or "who would want that?". Thomas Edison said talking pictures were not practical as people wanted quiet in the movie theaters. The New York Times in 1939 said that the average American family does not have time to sit and keep its eyes glued to a television screen.

In 1796, Edward Jenner proved that a cowpox vaccination could give protection against smallpox. The Royal Society refused to publish his paper as they thought this would destroy his good reputation. Some people thought going to the moon was too expensive and of no practical value. Democracy was ridiculed as rule by the mob.

Judge ideas by whether they are workable or unworkable.

As you create, you will judge. Judging too early in the creation process blocks creativity. Stop thinking of an idea as good or bad. A better way to look at an idea is whether it is useable. If it is useable, you have got something.   If it is not useable, you have three choices.

1. You can put the idea aside until you are ready to go to choices two or three. Your idea may be unworkable because the necessary technology is not available, or because people are not ready for it. We took a long time to accept the dishwasher. Josephine Cochrane invented it in the 1880's. It was well-designed as it won an award at the 1893 Chicago World Fair for "the best mechanical construction, durability, and adaptation to its line of work". Still housewives did not want a dishwasher. Ms. Cochrane's polls showed of all the housework, women liked washing dishes at the end of the meal as a relaxing chore.   Dishwashers did not start to become popular until the 1950's.

2. You can improve or fix the idea, as Cecil Booth did with the vacuum cleaner. He saw a demonstration of a "dust-removing machine". But instead of sucking up the dirt, it blew the dust out of the carpet with compressed air. Dust billowed everywhere, and some of it was picked up in a dust collector at the top of the machine. Booth thought of reversing the process and using suction. He mulled over the idea and suddenly decided to try it out on the plush chair in the restaurant where he was dining. He put his handkerchief on the back of his chair and sucked. He choked on the dust, but he knew suction worked when he saw the black outline of his mouth on his kerchief. He turned an unworkable idea into a workable one.

3. You can apply the idea to another field. Borrowing discoveries is a creativity tool. If your idea does not work here, maybe it will work somewhere else. At the end of the 19th century, Joshua Cowen had a novelty item called "the

166 Creating Ideas   Alice Steinbart

electric flowerpot". It was a flowerpot with a tube in the middle and a light bulb at the end, to light up the plant. It did not sell. But his employee, Conrad Hubert, had the insight to take the tube out, and use it as a flashlight. He founded the Eveready Flashlight Company and became rich. A silly idea became a good one.

You will come up with any number of ideas that will meet with opposition, often from yourself. A common reaction is "it can't be any good if I thought of it" or "if it's a good idea someone else would have thought of it". This is simply low self-esteem. I cannot begin to deal with the ravages of low self-esteem in this book. But there are many motivational books, seminars, and tapes that are available.

And how do you know your idea is a bad idea? The inventor of the glue for Post-it notes was looking for a super-glue. What good was this glue that would not stick, but peeled off? Definitely a failure. But he was open-minded enough to use The Stretch Tool to look for what uses this could have. And it became one of 3M's most successful sellers.

Once you have produced your creative idea, it's up to you to get it accepted. This is where most ideas are lost. There are any number of examples where someone came up with an idea, but did not follow it up. It had to be re-discovered or re-created later. Leonardo da Vinci conceived of a helicopter. Yet this is considered to be a 20th century invention. Alexander Fleming is credited with the discovery of penicillin in the 1920's. Yet there is documented evidence it was discovered in the 1800's, but nothing was done with it. How many people died because the earlier discoverer gave up?

Getting an idea accepted takes a different type of knowledge or creativity from coming up with the idea in the first place. We are all creative, but we are not all creative in the same fields. Remember Einstein could not write Shakespeare. You can create an idea, but it may take selling or marketing skills to get it accepted. If you do not have these skills and you do not want to learn them, you may need to turn your idea over to someone who does. If you do not, your idea may go nowhere, even though it is a good one.

There is hostility to creativity in our society. You hear "it can't be a good idea if I (you) thought of it (who are you?)" and "I can't do that." You are right. These tools will not work if you see yourself as non-creative. You will simply block yourself.

The belief that creativity is the province of geniuses, artists, scientists and inventors, that it's not common is more hostility to creativity. It relegates creativity to the few lucky or the rare gifted. It does not belong to us, the many. It's a similar analogy to asking whether you are a runner. "No," you reply, "the last time I competed in try-outs was in high-school" or "No, I don't like getting up early in the morning and running miles before breakfast". But if you have ever moved your legs and arms in a co-ordinated effort to go faster than a walk, you have run and are a runner. You may not be a marathoner or of Olympic caliber, but you can still run. And so it is with your creativity. You may not be a famous scientist or artist, and you may not see yourself as being creative, but everyone is. Because creativity is as simple as doing or thinking something you never did or thought before, even if someone else has. Putting creative people on a pedestal in admiration and saying "I am not like that" is doing a real disservice to yourself and to the proliferation of creativity in society. Everyone is creative and we are all capable of producing useful and workable ideas. Whether they are Nobel Prize winning or not.

Ideas are created daily. No one knows which ideas will be accepted or will be the money-makers, moving civilization along. History is replete with examples of good ideas discarded or opposed. There is a time lag between an idea being discovered and being accepted. Sometimes it takes centuries, sometimes decades, sometimes merely years. Did you know television was first shown to the public in 1936? But people only started buying t.v.'s in the 1950's.

Creating an idea is only the first step. The next is getting it accepted. That's a different topic altogether; partly marketing, partly tenacity, partly confidence, partly personal qualities such as the ability to co-operate and work with others, flexibility to change your beliefs as the world demands.

How well an idea does depends on the zest with which it is pursued and the ability with which it is marketed, not on how good an idea it is. Sticking with your creative idea in the face of opposition is your responsibility. Sometimes, if the idea is of particular value, it is a sacred trust. You must pursue it or humankind will be the loser. Putting your creative idea into practice may not be easy. But creativity is fun, financially rewarding, and absolutely essential.

The Dangerous Stages

There are two stages in the creative process that are destructive to creativity: before and after. Too many people subscribe to the myths "I am not creative" and "creativity occurs by happenstance". So they will not try, or they will stop too early, or they will give up on ideas they have created.

The match is a story of lost opportunity. In 1826, John Walker, of England, was mixing chemicals in an experiment to find a new explosive. Some of the mixture dried on his wooden stirring stick. He struck the stick on the floor to remove the stuff. It burst into flames. He showed his sticks off as toys, but he never patented them or manufactured them for sale. One of his audience did; Samuel Jones saw one of the demonstrations and he went into business selling matches.

The implementation stage, after you have created an idea, is the second dangerous time for creativity. We get lots of training in negative "what's wrong" and "it can't be done" thinking. When presented with a new idea, most people look for the flaws, at how it will not work, and at how much it costs. Of course, they will find problems, because nothing is perfect, there is always room for improvement. Everything we use and rely on, and all the ideas we hold, can be improved in some way. We can find something wrong with everything. This is not a reason to discard an idea. Unfortunately, the answer negative-thinking people give to a deficiency in your idea is to drop it.

You need to look for can-do people when you make your ideas public. These are the problem-solvers, not the problem-finders. They are the ones who will make an idea work. They are the people who have been responsible for all the progress we have ever made. These are the people who will accept your ideas.

Ideas are endless

Ideas are endless. We have millions of associations and experiences in our heads. If you take the numbers 1, 2, and 3, you can put them together in different orders. You can produce 321, and 312, and 231, and 213, and so on. And if you add a new stimulus, a new association, a new experience, the number 4, then you can generate all sorts of new sequences or thoughts. You can now have 4321, or 1432, and so on. Every time you add a new experience or piece of knowledge, you are increasing exponentially your ability to create something else.

Happenstance

So you think creativity is happenstance. "Look at the discovery of penicillin," you say, "Fleming accidently discovered it when one of his cultures grew a mold." The growing of the mold was happenstance; the discovery was not. Fleming was using The Hawk-eyes Tool. He paid attention to what was happening, noticing and asking questions. That was the creativity. That's not happenstance, but very controllable, if you choose to use The Hawk-eyes Tools. You are surrounded right now by any number of occurrences (like the growing of the mold) which could stimulate a creative idea, if you paid attention. Paying attention is controllable, not happenstance.

Technology

Sometimes technology has to catch up for us to make the next development. What would you do if you had a tin can, but no can opener? For over 60 years, people were stuck in this position. Tin cans were first developed in Britain in 1810. But the cans were large containers, often made of iron, not the light-weight tin we know. A can-opener would not be heavy-duty enough to open this strong cannister. Cans were used by the military, and soldiers used bayonets or pocket knives to open them. They were not for household use. In fact, one can from that era was marked "cut around the top with chisel and hammer". Not until the thinner cans of steel were manufactured in the 1850's could a can-opener be invented or be of use.

Since knowledge is advancing so quickly, the possibilities of creating more are increasing. Remember everything is connected. Shopping centers, drive-in restaurants (which have developed into fast food restaurants), supermarkets, all depended upon the development of the family car. So the more we have, the more we will create. There are more things to improve, to apply to another field, to add onto or change, to connect with something else to make something new. One thing leads to another. In fact, we are just getting started. Creating more leads to creating more still. Creativity is revved-up.

Creativity

You were creative when you were a child, before you went to school. That "you" is still there, hidden. You let that part of you out sometimes, when you are at play or at ease. It's the unfettered you, the part of you that likes being free, discovering, having fun, the part of you that finds creativity appealing. On those occasions when we do create, we are proud of our creations and of ourselves. We know it is unique and we are special. This is our creation. It may well be part of our legacy. We all have our contribution to make. It is for us to decide if we will let our creativity be stifled by the old, hostile thinking of "you're not creative".

This book gives you the tools to be creative at will. It is up to you what you do with them. Some people leave their tools out in the rain to get rusty. Others use their tools to build themselves a mansion. What will you do with yours?

The Tools

The Preparation Tools
The Detective Tool—ask questions

The Flip Tool—change the question

The Rebel Tool—list your assumptions

The Start-up Tools
The Humour Tool—laugh at your favourite comedian

The Silly Tool—be bizarre

The Organizational Tool
The Organizer Tool—mind mapping or clustering

The Right-Brain Tools
The Relaxing Tool—slow down your brain waves

The Incubation Tool—incubate

The Left-Brain Logical Tools
The Stubborn Tool—persist

The Explorer Tool—ask what if...

The Break Apart Tool—take it apart and put it together differently

The Left-Brain Lateral Tools

The Change Tool—change a characteristic

The Impossible Tool—what can't be done?

The Contrary Tool—mismatch

The Borrowing Tools

The Combining Tool—combine the first two things
   you see

The Booty Tool—take an idea from another field

The Mind Jar Tool—pick a noun or verb

The Role-playing Tool—what would another
   person do?

The Opinion Tool—ask others' opinions

The Hawk-eyes Tool—pay attention

The Improvement Tools

The Valuable Tool—every idea has something of
   value

The Garbage Tool—every idea has something less
   valuable.

The Check-up Tool—every idea can be improved

The Stretch Tool—find a dozen more uses

<u>Bibliography</u>

Bransford, John, Barry Stein, The Ideal Problem Solver: A Guide for Improving Thinking, Learning, and Creativity, W. H. Freeman and Company, 2nd edition, 1993.

de Bono, Edward, Lateral Thinking, Penguin Books, 1977.

de Bono, Edward, Serious Creativity, HarperCollins, 1993.

Fobes, Richard, The Creative Problem Solver's Toolbox: A Complete Course in the Art of Creating Solutions to Problems of Any Kind, Solutions Through Innovation, 1993.

Herrmann, Ned, The Creative Brain, The Ned Herrmann Group, 2nd edition, 1989.

Panati, Charles, Panati's Extraordinary Origin of Everyday Things, Perennial Library, 1987.

Perkins, D. N., The Mind's Best Work, Harvard University Press, 1992.

Thompson, Charles, What a Great Idea!, Harper Perennial, 1992.

Wonder, Jacquelyn, and Priscilla Donovan, The Flexibility Factor, Doubleday, 1989.

About the Author

Creating Brilliant Ideas is a eureka, a marriage of two happenings. The author's father, Ronald Steinbart, is a creative improviser. If anything breaks, the family takes it to him. He cobbles something workable together. It's handy having someone like him around. But what happens if he is not there. Then I am faced with a choice. I do without or I do it myself. "If he can fix it, why can't I? How would he do it?" So came the first realization; I too, can be a creative improviser.

The second occurrence came when Alice listened to a tape by Dr. Edward de Bono on The Six Thinking Hats. "Put on your creative thinking hat," he said. But how do you do that? Telling a person to be creative is much like telling someone "don't worry". Logical to say, but of no help if they don't know how. So Alice set about to find out. She developed the tools for Creating Brilliant Ideas.

Alice now presents workshops on how to create ideas and gives motivational speeches. To arrange a workshop or speech call:

phone toll free: 1-(877)-947-1475
fax: 1-(204)-956-1308
or write: 207-10 Fort St., Winnipeg,
                 Manitoba, Canada, R3C 1C4.

Tool Box

The Tool Box is a distillation of the essential elements of the book, plus all the tools as well as some ingredients for your Mind Jar. On one side is the graphic of the tool in colour, and on the other is a description of how the tool works and how to use it.

It is your summary of how to create ideas at will. You can carry it with you; a convenient, concise, and complete compendium.

The Detective Tool
This is one of The Preparation Tools.

Ask Questions.

Who?   What?

When?   Where?

Why?   How?

Is this the right question?

...stion or perceive
...nto a box just as
...trap. The answer
...question you ask.
...nking into new
...s.
...to ask the basic
...when, why, and
...rt-hand for many
...eds this, who else
...ation to help me,
...summarize all the
...then list all the
...From your rough
...ollow a theme, or
...e the question to
...the question is
...ly to another tool
...se ideas to The

There are two requirements to get into flow:

Flow.
Focus or concentration.
Passion or interest.

...there must be no
...passionate about
...concentrated on it,
...away and you have
...get you into flow.
...ction. You will get
...e distraction, or by
...terest becomes so
...distraction, so that
...u interest.
...u are concentrating
...est for you, you are
...ntent. Take away
...ow. Passion can
...et you past the
...ons are too strong,

For workshops and consultations, call
Alice Steinbart
207-10 Fort St., Winnipeg
Manitoba, Canada, R3C 1C4
phone toll free: 1-(877)-947-1475
fax: 1-(204)-957-1308

Order form

I would like to order _____ copies of Creating Ideas
at $16.95 per copy. (In Canada--$23.95)
I would like to order _____ Tool Box(es) at $29.95
per box. (In Canada $39.95)

Sub-total $_____

Shipping (per book $3.00-Canada $5.00)   _____

      (per Tool Box $6.50-Canada $8.50) _____

G.S.T. (Canada only) 7%   _____

G.S.T. No. R108478389

Total $_____

Name:_____

Address:_____

City:_____

State or Province:_____

Code:_____

Payment:

☐   Cheque   ☐   Money Order

☐   Credit Card: ☐   Visa   ☐   Mastercard

Card Number:_____

Name on card:_____Expiry date:_____

For workshops and consultations, call
Alice Steinbart
207-10 Fort St., Winnipeg
Manitoba, Canada, R3C 1C4
phone toll free: 1-(877)-947-1475
fax: 1-(204)-957-1308

Order Form

I would like to order _____ copies of Creating Ideas
at $16.95 per copy. (In Canada--$23.95)

I would like to order _____ Tool Box(es) at $29.95
per box. (In Canada $39.95)

Sub-total $_____

Shipping (per book $3.00-Canada $5.00)   _____

    (per Tool Box $6.50-Canada $8.50)   _____

G.S.T. (Canada only) 7%   _____

G.S.T. No. R108478389

Total $_____

Name:_____

Address:_____

City:_____

State or Province:_____

Code:_____

Payment:

☐   Cheque   ☐   Money Order

☐   Credit Card: ☐   Visa   ☐   Mastercard

Card Number:_____

Name on card:_____Expiry date:_____